HOMER: THE ILIAD

T0316277

Classical World Series

Classical World Series

HOMER: THE ILIAD

William Allan

B L O O M S B U R Y

LONDON • NEW DELHI • NEW YORK • SYDNEY

Bloomsbury Academic
An imprint of Bloomsbury Publishing Plc

50 Bedford Square   175 Fifth Avenue
London   New York
WC1B 3DP   NY 10010
UK   USA

www.bloomsbury.com

First published in 2012
Reprinted 2013

British Library Cataloguing-in-Publication Data
A catalogue record for this book is available from the British Library.

ISBN: HB: 978-1-8496-6889-7

Library of Congress Cataloging-in-Publication Data
A catalog record for this book is available from the Library of Congress.

Typeset by Ray Davies

Contents

For Laura

Preface

In its narrative skill and characterization, its use of language and the richness of its imaginative world, there is nothing quite like the *Iliad* in all of classical literature. Given the circumstances of its composition in archaic Greece, it is a miracle that the poem has survived; but given the artistic genius behind it, it is an even greater miracle that it was ever created at all. We have a lot to thank the Muses for.

This book seeks to offer a clear and stimulating introduction to Homer's *Iliad*, suitable for undergraduate students of Greek or Classical Civilization, and pupils in the upper forms of schools. It will also be of interest, I hope, to other students of literature and history, and to the general reader.

In order to maximize its usefulness to students, the book is organized around the core topics most regularly covered in courses on the poem (whether in Greek or in translation): the genre of epic, the style and structure of the *Iliad*, the nature of heroism, the role of the gods, and finally the ethics of war and its impact on family life and gender roles. All references (e.g. 1.231) are to the *Iliad*, unless otherwise stated (e.g. *Odyssey* 6.180-5). The book contains no plot summary of the *Iliad*, but assumes the reader has already read the poem itself; after all, there is nothing better.

I am grateful to Roger Rees for asking me to contribute to this series, to Deborah Blake at Bloomsbury Academic for her advice and assistance, and to Adrian Kelly, Roger Rees, and Laura Swift for their insightful comments on a draft of the book. The book is dedicated, with love and *homophrosynê*, to my wife Laura.

W.R.A.
University College, Oxford
November 2011

EUXINE SEA

Heraclea

Bosphorus

Byzantium

B i t h y n i a

Nicomedia

Propontis

Ancyra

Nicaea

Cyzicus

Hellespont

Ilios

Pergamum

A S I A   M I N O R

Caesarea

Sardis

Apamea

Smyrna

I o n i a

Ephesus

Sagalassos

Laodicea

Samos

Priene

Miletus

Perge

Halicarnassus

Cos

Xanthus

Cnidos

Rhodes

Greece and Asia Minor

Chapter 1

Homer and Early Greek Epic

As well as outlining the historical background to Homer's poems, this chapter will examine early Greek epic as a genre, with particular emphasis on the *Iliad* as a traditional oral (or oral-derived) poem. We will therefore consider some of the most fundamental questions in the study of ancient Greek literature: What is epic? Who was Homer? And what did Homer do with the epic tradition that he inherited?

Epic derives from the Greek word *epos*, meaning 'word', and in the broadest terms refers to any poetry written in dactylic hexameters (for this metrical scheme see Chapter 2 below). Thus the *Works and Days* counts as epic, a poem on self-improvement and honest work written by Hesiod (a near contemporary of Homer's) in the early seventh century BC, but it is usually categorized as 'didactic epic' to distinguish it from what became the canonical form of the genre, that is, hexameter narrative poetry dealing with divine and heroic myth. The serious subject-matter of such poetry (war and death, gods and heroes, and so on), combined with Homer's unique status as the best of poets, ensured that epic became, within the ancient hierarchy of genres, the premier literary form. Moreover, the Homeric epics not only exerted a profound influence on later literature, myth, and art, but also shaped the ethical and religious beliefs of the Greeks for many centuries to come, and were the basis of early Greek education throughout antiquity. The speakers in Plato's *Republic*, for example, take it for granted that Homer is 'the poet who has educated Greece' (606e): his cultural authority was unparalleled.

Most societies have a form of poetry resembling Greek epic, that is, tales of the gods and of powerful men and women from the past, though their precise form and expression differ from culture to culture. Greek epic is defined formally (recited rhythmically by a solo singer) and thematically (dealing with events from the distant heroic age). The word used by Homer to describe these heroic stories is *oimê*, meaning 'path', referring to the 'path of song' which the poet (and his audience) would travel along; in the *Odyssey*, for example, the bard Demodocus at one point selects the *oimê* of the quarrel of Odysseus and Achilles (8.73-6), moving Odysseus himself to tears. In other words, the poet, whose authority is guaranteed by the Muses (note the invocation of the Muse in the opening lines of both *Iliad* and *Odyssey*), plots his own 'path' through the forests of Greek heroic myth, and his audience admire his skill in doing so. The raw material or subject-matter of these 'paths' is the *klea andrôn*, or 'tales of men's glory', whose fame the poet celebrates and continues. Both Homeric epics show a clear awareness of their place in this tradition of heroic song: Achilles sings the *klea andrôn* as he sulks in his hut (9.189), while Helen laments that she and Paris will be the subject of song for generations to come (6.357-8). And it is no coincidence that the central heroes of both epics, Achilles and Odysseus, are compared to bards, as when, for example, Odysseus stringing his bow is likened to a bard stringing his lyre (*Odyssey* 21.406-11). Like any other itinerant poet, reliant on the financial support of patron and audience, Homer takes care to advertise his own skill. The bard Phemius in the *Odyssey*, pleading for his life, emphasizes that such skill comes through hard practice as well as divine favour: 'I am self-taught, and god has put in my mind every pathway [*oimê*] of song' (22.347-8).

There is, at first sight, a remarkable puzzle at the heart of western literature: Homer is arguably the greatest poet who ever lived and yet we know nothing about him. It is clear that the ancients knew nothing certain about him either, although such was his renown that many different places (several Ionian cities of the Asia Minor coast and east Aegean islands, especially Chios, Smyrna, Colophon, and Cyme) claimed to be where he was born, lived, or died, none of them convincingly. However, this mystery in fact turns out to be entirely deliberate, as there is a very good reason why the poet avoids connection with any one place: for rather than being a specific person with a particular biography, the faceless poet becomes a conduit of divine inspiration whose authority is universal. Once again, a comparison with Hesiod is helpful, for whereas Hesiod in the *Works and Days* emphasizes the value of his poetry by constructing a particular persona and personal history (namely, a Boeotian farmer with a wastrel brother who had better listen to his advice), so Homer effaces his own identity (and even his name) in order to assert his quasi-divine poetic authority.

But although we do not know who Homer was, it is clear that there is a single creative intelligence behind each poem. Many modern scholars believe that the *Iliad* poet and the *Odyssey* poet are different people (for a variety of linguistic, theological, and geographical reasons), and this view was held in antiquity, albeit by a small minority. However, as with the identity of Homer (whose poems we can enjoy and interpret without knowing any 'facts' about him), the question of whether he is one person or two is much less important than it seems. For all that really matters is the *Iliad* and *Odyssey* themselves and their shaping by a master poet or poets, who (for the sake of convenience) we will call Homer.

In turning to the texts we are faced with the perennial 'Homeric question', that is, the debate over the origins and early transmission of the poems. The scholarly debates here go around endlessly (fuelled by the lack of evidence), and one is left feeling at times like Mark Twain's schoolboy that 'Homer was not written by Homer, but by another man of that name.' In truth, unless we suddenly find an eighth- or seventh-century BC manuscript of Homer (an unlikely scenario), no definitive answer is possible, and we have to admit that the precise manner in which the *Iliad* was composed and recorded cannot be known for sure. All we can do is set out some more or less likely scenarios, given what we can reconstruct about the tradition of epic poetry in archaic Greece. Similarly, we have only approximate dates for the Homeric epics: they show familiarity with features such as writing, temples, cult statues, narrative art, and a wide knowledge of Mediterranean geography, which suggest they cannot be earlier than the second half of the eighth century BC, while allusions to Homer in the poet Archilochus (note in particular the new Telephus fragment of Archilochus, dealing with the Achaeans' mistaken attack on Mysia rather than Troy, first published in 2005) suggest that the *Iliad* was familiar to audiences by 650 BC at the latest, when Archilochus was active.

So, assuming that the poems were composed and disseminated some time between 725 and 650 BC, we must ask when they were first written down: was this done in the poet's lifetime or at some point after (perhaps long after) their composition? While all viable answers to the Homeric question recognize that the Homeric epics are products of an oral poetic tradition (see Chapter 2 below for the typical techniques of oral composition), they differ in the way they integrate writing and literacy into their account of the poem's creation and ultimate survival. So let us consider three of the most plausible scenarios: first, that Homer himself wrote the poems down; secondly, that he dictated them, being himself illiterate; and thirdly, that the poems were memorized by bards for several generations and written down later.

Although Homer uses the compositional techniques developed by illiterate bards over many centuries, that does not prove he was himself unable to read or write. The Greeks had adapted their alphabet (with local variations) from a Phoenician source around 800 BC and the earliest surviving inscriptions date from roughly 740. So, if he was literate, Homer would be among the first generations of Greeks to use the new technology of alphabetic writing. (The poet reflects his largely illiterate audience's mixture of wonder at, and suspicion of, this new technology in the *Iliad*'s only reference to writing, when the orders to execute the bearer of a missive are described as 'deadly signs, many fatal marks written in a folded tablet' (6.168-9).) Using a reed pen and a black carbon-based ink, he could have written his poems on papyrus (more likely than animal-skins, because cheaper and less bulky; a ship's cable made of papyrus is mentioned at *Odyssey* 21.391), creating a large set of papyrus rolls (each roll could hold approximately 1500 lines of verse, i.e. two to three books of the *Iliad*). In this scenario Homer remains an essentially oral poet, but one who uses writing to aid the development of his work, using the time between performances to write down his poem and add to it over many years.

Scholars sometimes argue that oral poets never write themselves, but this is dogma rather than fact and is disproved by comparative evidence from other cultures with oral poetic traditions. The problem with 'hard' oralism of this kind is that it sets up too sharp a divide between orality and literacy, as if Homer's learning to read and write inevitably obliterated his chances of picking up the traditional skills of epic composition and performance. On the contrary, it is possible (and perhaps a more attractive hypothesis) that an essentially oral poet who had learned to write might see the creative potential of this new medium, and use it to create something particularly sophisticated.

An alternative theory is that Homer himself never learned to read and write, but that he or a wealthy patron recognized the potential of the new technology, and Homer dictated his poem to a literate scribe in order to preserve it for posterity. Scholars who support this theory often suggest that it can account for the unusual length and sophistication of the Homeric poems, on the grounds that a poet forced to go slowly would be able to embellish and expand his song in a way that is said to be less likely in a live performance. However, this is to misunderstand the nature of oral composition, which allows a bard to develop his material over multiple performances and which is in fact designed to facilitate such large-scale pieces (on this issue see Chapter 2 below). Moreover, the dictation theory has its own problems: most notably, could a poet used to live performance keep up the flow of his poetry if forced to recite at a snail's pace?

Finally, let us consider the idea that the poems were memorized and transmitted orally for several generations until writing became more established. Here too comparative evidence suggests that bards would modify the poem in reperformance, introducing their own innovations, so that the poems would change, often in significant ways. Moreover, the language of the poems stops changing in Homer's time, which suggests extremely accurate memorization (if not early fixation in written texts). So we need people capable of memorizing long texts, which in itself is not a problem in a predominantly oral culture (books were rare and expensive well into the fifth century BC). And here we may distinguish between creative oral poets or bards (*aoidoi*) and rhapsodes ('song-stitchers'): the latter memorized poems created by others and recited them in public performance. Indeed we are told of a guild of rhapsodes called the Homeridae ('sons of Homer') dedicated to the preservation of the great master's works. But we cannot be sure that rhapsodes were not reliant on written texts.

In conclusion, there is not enough evidence to settle the 'Homeric question' decisively, but on balance it seems likely that the poems were preserved in written form in the poet's own lifetime. After all, writing did exist, so why wait several generations to use it? And if we ask what could have triggered the major decision to preserve such large poems in writing, the answer is simple: quality. For we have enough fragments of other early Greek epic (for example, the poems of the so-called Epic Cycle or the *Shield of Heracles* attributed to Hesiod) to know that there is a huge gap in quality between the Homeric epics and those of other poets. (Other poems originally attributed to Homer were gradually stripped away on the grounds of quality, so that by the fourth century BC only the *Iliad* and *Odyssey* were believed to be genuine.) The existence and partial survival of these other works do show that there was a market for other kinds of poetry (from the episodic, pack-everything-in style of the Epic Cycle to the macabre 'pulp' epic of the *Shield of Heracles*), but they also underline how exceptional the *Iliad* and *Odyssey* are, and how amazed their first audiences must have been by them.

The Homeric epics, then, are transitional poems, in the sense that they are products of an oral tradition, but achieved their final form when writing was known and spreading. Of course we experience the poems today as written texts, and their popularity throughout antiquity ensured that they have come down to us in reasonably good condition. (Book 10 of the *Iliad*, the so-called *Doloneia* or 'killing of Dolon', and a few other short passages were inserted later.) But that is not how they were enjoyed by their original (archaic Greek) audiences: the Homeric epics were composed for live performance, and even if Homer was literate, he learned his craft from other performing bards. He will have developed his poems over many years of performance, usually delivering short episodes rather than the entire work. The *Iliad* would take around 26 hours to perform in its entirety, and although it is quite possible that some patrons and audiences were willing to set aside several days for such a performance (after all, fifth-century BC Athenians were happy to sit through three days of tragedy and satyr play at the city's main theatrical festival, the Great Dionysia, and modern Wagner fans spend four nights on the Ring Cycle), it will have been a less common event in the career of a travelling poet than shorter one-off shows.

This is reflected in the poems themselves, which lend themselves to performance in single-session chunks (e.g. the Quarrel in Book 1, the duel of Paris and Menelaus in 3, the meeting of Hector and Andromache in Book 6, and so on), which the audience can appreciate in their own right, especially when they know the general shape of the story from other performances. We see similar shorter songs performed by Phemius and Demodocus in the *Odyssey*. They are court poets, attached to particular royal families, whereas Homer is likely to have been itinerant, performing in a variety of contexts: the halls of wealthy chieftains (especially after feasts, as in the *Odyssey*), but also at weddings, funerals, and public festivals of various kinds. As with his own identity, Homer is deliberately silent about the performance context of his poetry, and for similar reasons: for he wants his work to be as universal as possible, so that it appeals not to one specific family, clan, or city but to all Greek-speaking communities. In that way Homer can perform all over the Greek world, making his poems more portable, flexible, and profitable. Moreover, the poetic performances that followed funerals or formed the centrepiece of many public festivals were *contests*, and this leads us to a basic feature of early Greek epic whose importance must not be overlooked: poets were often competing against one another (whether for prizes or to attract future patronage). As a result, not only would 'bard begrudge bard' (as Hesiod puts it, *Works and Days* 26), but there was great pressure on each poet to continually innovate and improve his song if he was to keep impressing his audiences.

How was this achieved? After all, the poet would not necessarily know how long he had to perform or what episode his audience would want to hear, so he had to be able to tailor his performance to their wishes. Scholars often speak of the poet 'improvising' his song, but this term is misleading insofar as it suggests a poet who makes up his material anew each time. The bard will have honed certain scenes and episodes over many performances in the past, as well as practising and revising them between performances. Using that material, as well as his memorized store of formulae and story patterns (see Chapter 2 below), the skilled bard will create a song which is 'made new' each time as he reacts to the needs of the occasion and his audience. This process of 'composition in performance' is extemporaneous, but also premeditated, since it is shaped by the bard's traditional forms of expression and his adaptation of older material. So there is no opposition between tradition and invention in Homeric poetry; both are part of the craft of oral composition, where the bard needs the tradition to build upon. And the tradition is also central to the audience's pleasure in the poetry, since the bard will use their knowledge of epic themes and characters from previous performances in order to enrich their appreciation of his work. It is the audience who judge a bard's success, and his goal is to induce in them *thelxis* or *kêlêthmos*, a state of spellbound exaltation.

Having considered Homer's performance context, let us now try to situate the *Iliad* within the wider tradition of early Greek epic, showing how it engages with and transforms both Trojan and other myth. Here too Homer's vast inherited tradition, far from being a hindrance, emerges as the dynamo of his creativity and innovation. It is clear that Homer knew many other heroic tales beyond the Trojan War. Indeed such wide knowledge was essential to his craft as a traditional oral poet; we may recall Phemius' boast that 'god has put in my mind every pathway [*oimê*] of song' (*Odyssey* 22.347-8). Besides the Trojan War the other major war of the heroic age was that against Thebes, and Homer alludes to it on several occasions. Diomedes, one of the foremost Achaean warriors at Troy, had succeeded in sacking Thebes, whereas his father Tydeus had died during the first campaign. Diomedes' earlier success is used to rebut Agamemnon's charge of cowardice against him (4.370-410), and throughout the poem Diomedes is keen to live up to his father's heroic achievements (5.802-8, 6.222-3, 14.113-14, 126-7). But Theban references are not limited to Diomedes and Tydeus: the poet recalls, for example, Funeral Games for Oedipus at Thebes (23.679-80). Another body of (non-Trojan) heroic myth was centred on Pylos, whose aged king Nestor is present at Troy and who never misses an opportunity to remind the Achaeans of his former prowess (e.g. 7.132-56, 11.670-761, 23.629-45). Homer is also familiar with heroic tales relating to Thessaly: the wedding of Peleus and Thetis (24.59-63), the war of the Lapiths and Centaurs (1.260-73), and the expedition of Jason and the Argonauts (7.467-9). Finally, there are numerous references to Heracles, one of the most famous of heroes, covering his birth (14.323-4), his labours (8.362-9, 15.638-40), and his death (18.117-19). Significantly, the episode in Heracles' life most frequently referred to is his sacking of Laomedon's Troy after being cheated by the Trojan king (5.638-54, 14.249-51, 20.144-8). This example of earlier Trojan deceit, relevant to the Trojans' conduct in the *Iliad*, reminds us that these allusions to other epic tales always have a point within the *Iliad* itself: Homer is not simply showing off his knowledge of Greek myth but using it to enhance his own story.

We see a similar process in the poem's use of Trojan War myth. Although the *Iliad* recounts only four days of actual fighting in the tenth year of the war, Homer deploys references to the wider Trojan myth throughout. Thus we are told of various earlier events, including the Judgement of Paris (24.25-30), the abduction of Helen (e.g. 3.173-5, 442-5), the gathering of forces at Aulis (2.303-29), and the failed embassy of Menelaus and Odysseus to Troy (3.205-24, 11.123-5, 138-42). From the period after the *Iliad* ends the poet alludes to the death of Achilles at the hands of Paris and Apollo (22.358-60), the arrival of Philoctetes at Troy (2.724-5), the sack of Troy (12.10-15, 15.69-71), and Aeneas' rule over the surviving Trojans (20.302-8). Trojan War myth was also the subject of six poems in the later Epic Cycle (seventh and sixth centuries BC); these took care to fit around the Homeric epics, creating a history of the heroic age from the start of the war to the death of Odysseus, in the sequence *Cypria*, **Iliad**, *Aethiopis*, *Little Iliad*, *Sack of Troy*, *Returns*, **Odyssey**, *Telegony*. The surviving fragments and summaries of these poems, with their inclusion of the more fantastic aspects of myth (magical armour, monsters, invulnerable and immortal fighters), throw into relief Homer's more austere vision of the heroic world, especially in the *Iliad*. It is not clear to what extent they embody Trojan material which would have existed in Homer's time (rather than being written later under his influence), but their survival reminds us that it is an essential part of Homer's skill as a poet to engage with the other stories that make up the epic universe known to both him and his audience.

As well as alluding to other stories, Homer can introduce his own innovations, changing the myths, and even inventing new ones, to suit his plot and characters. Thus in the first book of the *Iliad* Achilles reminds Thetis of an attempt by Hera, Poseidon, and Athena to overthrow Zeus (1.396-406), a myth not attested elsewhere, but well suited to its context here, since Zeus' debt to Thetis (she had loosed the bonds put on him by the other gods) will persuade him to grant her request to aid the Trojans until the Achaeans show respect to Achilles. Homer has deliberately chosen the three gods (Hera, Poseidon, and Athena) who are most likely to be opposed to Thetis' request, since they are passionate enemies of the Trojans; his mythical innovation is thus skilfully interwoven with his plot. Similarly, in the final book of the *Iliad* Achilles urges the grieving Priam to eat, recalling the story of Niobe, who ate despite losing twelve children (24.601-19). The detail of Niobe's eating is a new element in the story, which usually focuses on Niobe's boasting of her many children, her punishment by the gods, and her transformation into a streaming rock on Mt Sipylus in Magnesia (all details retained by Achilles); once again the innovation is designed to suit its rhetorical context: like Niobe, Achilles argues, Priam should stop weeping and eat. Thus, as these examples (Trojan and non-Trojan) make clear, Homer's engagement with the larger story-hoard of Greek myth is a major part of his originality and skill. He exploits his audience's awareness of these earlier traditions to expand and enrich his own epic narrative, and introduces other tales, not willy-nilly, but always with a clear thematic purpose.

Moreover, despite his adaptation and invention of myth, the poet's account of the heroic past has a strong claim to truthfulness. For the Greeks believed that the heroic age had existed and that epic poets recorded their national past. An important hallmark of good poetry was its vividness and authenticity, as if the poet himself had witnessed the events. Thus Odysseus praises Demodocus 'above all men' because he sings of the Achaeans' deeds and sufferings 'as if you had been there yourself or heard the story from one who was' (*Odyssey* 487-9) – a real compliment, coming from one of those suffering Achaean heroes. The bard's superhuman knowledge is guaranteed by the Muses, whose importance to the Greek epic tradition is profound. Homer invokes the Muses at key points in his narrative, each time to justify his authority to sing of the distant past (e.g. 1.1-7, 2.761-2, 11.218-20, 14.508-10, 16.112-13); perhaps the best illustration of their importance comes at the start of the huge Catalogue of Ships in Book 2, where the poet justifies his need of them: 'for you are goddesses and are present and know everything, while we [mortals] hear only rumour and know nothing' (2.485-6). The Muses grant the poet's account the authority of fact and license his creativity.

But how historical is the poet's vision of the Trojan War? Did such an event even take place? When something like the writing of history as we know it was developed in the fifth century BC by Herodotus and Thucydides, the historians express doubts about Homer's reliability, often as a means of establishing their own historical authority and the superior interest of the wars they are writing about (whether Persian or Peloponnesian). Thus Thucydides claims that even if we can trust Homer's figures – 'and it is likely that, being a poet, he would exaggerate and embellish' – then the forces involved in the Trojan War were still smaller than those involved in the conflict recorded by Thucydides (1.10.3). And he has Pericles declare that the Athenians need no Homer to celebrate their achievements, the implication being that they now have Thucydides to do so (2.41.4). Nonetheless, both Herodotus and

Thucydides treat Homer as a valid historical source, albeit a poetic or mythicized one; and most strikingly, both believe (as did all Greeks) that the Trojan War actually took place.

Research on contact between Greece and the Near East in the late Bronze Age (thirteenth and early twelfth centuries BC) has shown that there is likely to be a historical core to the Greek epic tradition and its account of the fall of Troy. Surviving records from the Hittite capital of Hattusas (now Boghazköy in central Turkey) refer to a place called Wilusa or Wilusiya in north-western Asia Minor, which can be plausibly identified with Homer's Troy ((*W*)*Ilios* in Greek). These records also mention a power called Ahhiyawa, which we can recognize as the land of Homer's Achaeans (*Achai(w)oi*). The picture that emerges from the Hittite documents is one of competition between the Hittite and Mycenaean kingdoms for control of various settlements on the Asia Minor coast, including Wilusa/Troy. Archaeology shows that Troy was attacked and destroyed several times during this period (*c.* 1270-1180 BC), and it is likely that Mycenaean Greeks were among the attackers. So there seems to be a historical kernel to the tale of Troy's destruction at the hands of Greeks.

However, despite the Greeks' belief in the reality of the Trojan War, when history becomes heroic poetry it inevitably becomes a form of fiction. And over the many centuries separating the conflicts of the late Bronze Age and Homer's own time bards will have continuously transformed their Trojan material to suit the needs of successive generations and audiences. Thus a conflict fought (one imagines) for complex military and political reasons became a war fought for a woman (Helen of Troy), while poetic exaggeration has left its mark throughout: 10 years of fighting, 1186 Achaean ships, and so on. Most pervasive is the effect of nostalgia for a bygone Heroic Age, which is a leitmotif of the Greek epic tradition, as seen, for example, in the Homeric warriors' physical superiority to men of today: 'A man could not easily lift that rock with both hands, even a very strong man, such as mortals now are' (12.381-3, said of Ajax, son of Telamon). This 'epic distance' between mundane present and heroic past is most explicit in the description of the destruction of the Achaean defensive wall by Poseidon and Apollo after the war has ended, where the poet looks back from his own time to the 'race of men half-divine' who fought at Troy (12.23). Such awe at the lineage and strength of the warriors, and at the scale of the expedition and the length of the war, lent the epic world an archaic grandeur, but also ensured its transformation of the 'historical' Trojan War into something much larger than life.

Yet for all its poetic embellishment, the Homeric world is not purely fiction, but a kind of historical amalgam with its own distinctive patterns or layers. Of course its primary audience is that of Homer's day (late eighth or early seventh century BC), and the story of the Trojan War has been reshaped to suit their values and beliefs; as such it can tell us nothing about actual Mycenaean values or society. Nonetheless, it does preserve a few relics of earlier generations, reaching back to the Mycenaean Age itself: for example, Ajax's tower-like shield, the boar's-tusk helmet worn by Odysseus (10.261-5), Nestor's great cup (11.632-7), and the use of bronze (rather than iron) as the main metal for weapons. Though they are in a sense mere background to the main narrative and do not greatly affect its plot or characters, these fossilized memories of an earlier age are an essential part of the epic tradition's attempt to create a distinctively heroic world. Homer and his audiences may have known almost nothing about Mycenaean palace society or the reasons for its collapse around 1200 BC, but the period of relative decline which followed (including the loss of literacy, figurative drawing, and metalworking skills), not to mention the impressive ruins and tombs at places like Mycenae, Tiryns, and Pylos, will have encouraged the poets in their nostalgic evocation of a heroic past. Strikingly, Hera submits to the future destruction of her favourite cities, 'Argos, Sparta, and Mycenae of the wide streets' (as long as Zeus agrees to her demand for the destruction of Troy), exploiting the Homeric audience's awareness of the end of the Mycenaean world (4.51-3).

The epics also reflect another important feature of the cultural developments that took place between the late Bronze Age and Homer's time, namely, an interaction with Near Eastern story-telling and myth. The two main periods of cultural exchange were between 1450 and 1200 BC (during the Mycenaean period), then again in the eighth and seventh centuries BC. The latter period is sometimes referred to as 'the Orientalizing revolution' in Greek culture, but it is more a matter of intensity than an outright revolution, since Greeks and their Near Eastern neighbours were constantly interacting with one another throughout the so-called 'Dark Ages' (twelfth to ninth centuries BC, when literacy was lost). Eastern and Greek relations were channelled in various directions, but especially through the Phoenicians (via Cyprus) and through Lydia (in western Asia Minor). Migrant workers enabled the transference of stories across national boundaries, not just poets, but merchants, mercenaries, and craftsmen of all kinds (especially blacksmiths and jewellers); nor should we forget the countless oriental slaves, prostitutes, and refugees living in Greece. In the *Odyssey* the loyal swineherd Eumaeus speaks of migrants who are valued by their host community:

'those whose craft is for the public good – a seer, a healer of sickness, a carpenter, or indeed an inspired bard, who delights with his singing' (17.383-5). Since Greek was something of a *lingua franca* in the eastern Mediterranean from the ninth century BC onwards, travelling bards might encounter foreigners who knew Greek (or be bilingual themselves) and would be able to exchange stories from each other's traditions.

Thus the Greek oral tradition could potentially bring in wide influences, and some scholars have even argued for influence between specific oriental texts and Homer. So, for example, some see similarities between Achilles and Gilgamesh (hero of an eponymous Akkadian epic) – both have divine mothers and dear comrades (Patroclus, Enkidu) whose death devastates the hero and sends him on a quest – but the alleged 'parallels' are often rather tenuous (Achilles' quest is to kill Hector, Gilgamesh travels to the flood survivor Utnapishtim to learn the secret of eternal life), and they can be explained in terms of story patterns (such as revenge for the death of a companion) found across several cultures (e.g. Germanic and Japanese) which have had no significant contact. Moreover, even if we grant the possibility of specific influences, they are likely to have begun a long time before Homer and, most importantly, they will have been thoroughly adapted by generations of Greek bards to suit their very different context, namely, a Greek society which differed in numerous respects (moral, political, religious, etc.) from its Near Eastern neighbours. (The same principle applies to aspects of early Greek poetry that are shared with other Indo-European cultures, such as the hero's desire for fame even at the cost of his own life.) So it is unlikely that Homer or his audience will have seen Gilgamesh and Enkidu behind Achilles and Patroclus, since a bard's priority was to make sense to a Greek audience. In short, speculation about the distant 'origins' of motifs in Homer's poetry is much less illuminating than seeing what role these motifs play within the Greek epic tradition itself.

In conclusion, Homer inherited a rich and dynamic tradition of oral poetry, whose subjects and techniques he deployed to create the *Iliad*, the greatest of epic poems. The precise nature of those traditional oral-derived techniques will be the subject of our next chapter.

Chapter 2

Language, Style, and Structure

'Timeless' classic though it is, the *Iliad* is a product of a particular time and poetic culture, and this chapter will aim to illustrate that culture through specific examples. We shall see how the oral performance context of early Greek epic informs the style of the poem at every level, from simple noun-epithet combinations to the overall structure of the work itself. Features of the oral-derived style which may strike modern readers as unusual will be shown to aid (re)composition in performance, and various examples will illustrate the poet's skill in using repetition and variation, the basic techniques of oral poetry, to create meaning.

The Greek word for the bard's performance is *aoidê*, usually translated as 'song', although 'chant' would be more accurate. The 'singer' accompanied himself with a lyre (*kithara* or *phorminx*), as do Phemius and Demodocus in the *Odyssey* and Achilles in the *Iliad* (9.186-91). His music or melody (now lost) probably remained the same for each verse, but monotony was avoided by varying tones of delivery, especially when the performer 'acted' the various characters involved, lending them yet more vividness and credibility. The same metrical pattern (the dactylic hexameter) governs every verse, but the verses are not metrically identical, since the hexameter has a flexible structure, and can run from twelve to seventeen syllables in each verse. Unlike English verse, which is based on the pattern of stresses, ancient Greek metre was based on the opposition of long (marked as '–') and short ('∪') syllables. The dactylic hexameter consists of six dactylic metra or feet. Any of the first five feet can be a dactyl (– ∪ ∪) or spondee (– –), and the sixth foot a spondee or trochee (– ∪). So the pattern is

$$-\bar{\cup}\bar{\cup}\,|-\bar{\cup}\bar{\cup}\,|-\bar{\cup}\bar{\cup}\,|-\bar{\cup}\bar{\cup}\,|-\bar{\cup}\bar{\cup}\,|-\bar{\cup}$$

Thus the first line of the *Iliad*, *mênin aeide thea Pêlêïadeô Achilêos* ('Sing, goddess, of the anger of Achilles, son of Peleus'), scans as – ∪ ∪ | – ∪ ∪ | – – | – ∪ ∪ | – ∪ ∪ | – ∪. (Note that the two vowels *-eô* in *Pêlêïadeô* are here combined to make one long syllable, a process called *synecphonesis* or *synizesis*.) Spondees can replace dactyls in any of the first five feet, though this is very rare in the fifth foot (only 5% of verses) so that the end of the verse has a characteristic cadence ($- \cup \cup - -$). The hexameter also has a natural pause within each line, which can occur only at the end of a word. This word-end (or 'caesura') comes after the first long syllable of the third foot (as in the opening line of the *Iliad* above, after the long -*a* of *thea*), or between the two shorts there, or (much less commonly, around 2% of verses) after the first long syllable of the fourth foot. These regular word-breaks in the third foot mean that the line falls into two parts (or 'cola'), and many of the formulaic phrases of epic diction are designed to fit these cola, making them easier for the poet to combine in performance, as in *ton d' êmeibet' epeita* + *podarkês dios Achilleus*, i.e. 'and then he answered him' + 'swift-footed godlike Achilles' as the subject of the verb (1.121, Achilles rebuking Agamemnon). As nursery rhymes show, metre makes things more memorable, and the regular rhythms of Homeric formulas exploit that principle to the full.

The need to fit the metre is one of the reasons that Homeric Greek is an artificial language, with various forms from several different dialects and periods, which was never spoken by any real-life Greek community. Thus the word for 'day', for example, can be *hêmerê* (an Ionic form) or *êmar* (Arcado-Cypriot); the genitive singular (masculine, second declension) can end in the contemporary form -*ou* or the archaic -*oio*; or the poet can express 'to be' in five different ways (*einai, emen, emmen, emenai, emmenai*), all of these options designed to suit different metrical situations. The epic language, like the material world of the poem, was an amalgam of old and new, with even some remnants of Mycenaean Greek (such as first declension genitive plurals in -*aôn*). But of course the language could not be too abstruse or archaic since it had to be comprehensible in performance. The predominant dialect of the poem is Ionic, with an admixture of Aeolic forms to suit the metre (e.g. *ammes* for Ionic *hêmeis*, 'we'). This suggests that the most vigorous development of the epic tradition took place in the Ionic speaking communities of Asia Minor and the Ionian islands of the Aegean as far west as Euboea, but that early bards also performed in Aeolic speaking areas such as Boeotia and Thessaly and parts of Asia Minor including the island of Lesbos. Nonetheless, Homeric Greek was intelligible throughout the Greek world and its mixture of different dialects (though geared principally to metrical variety) added to its Panhellenic appeal. As usually happens in Greek literature, the dialect used by the best exponent of a genre became the standard one for it, so that Homer's basically Ionic diction was used by all subsequent epic poets regardless of where they came from.

As noted above, the metrical rhythm of Greek epic shapes its language, and the poet was able to deploy a large number of standard phrases to fit the metre. Such 'formulas' are found in *all* grammatical categories of epic diction, but the most striking is the combination of noun and epithet(s), as in 'swift-footed godlike Achilles', 'rosy-fingered dawn', 'Hector of the flashing helmet', and so on. In his pioneering work on Homeric poetry in the 1920s and 30s, Milman Parry showed that there was a system behind such expressions, and that this formulaic system was not the creation of a single poet, but the product of a long tradition of oral (re)composition in performance. Parry defined a 'formula' as 'a group of words which is regularly employed under the same metrical conditions to express a given essential idea', and he went on to show that there is just one formula for each particular character or action in any given position in the verse. This principle, which he called 'economy', can be seen, for example, in the way Hector is described in the nominative case in the second half of a Homeric verse: depending on how long an expression the poet needs to complete the line, Hector will be called 'glorious' (*phaidimos Hektôr*) or 'of the flashing helmet' (*koruthaiolos Hektôr*) or 'great Hector of the flashing helmet' (*megas koruthaiolos Hektôr*), and there is no other way to name him for each of these metrical units.

However, this does not make such phrases merely ornamental (i.e. with no more significance than the bare name 'Hector', as Parry's early studies concluded) since the epithets express important qualities of the characters concerned: for example, it is essential to Odysseus' identity and the stories told of him that he is 'much enduring' (*polutlas*) and 'of many wiles' (*polumêtis*). Moreover, the extent to which the audience's sensitivity to an epithet is activated depends on the context, which is shaped by the poet: thus in the phrase 'then Agamemnon, lord of men, answered him' the epithet 'lord of men' is fairly colourless, but in the context of the poem's opening lines, where the disastrous quarrel is located between 'Atreus' son, lord of men, and godlike Achilles' (1.7), the same epithet is charged with meaning, for it is precisely Agamemnon's fitness for the task of being 'lord of men' that will be the issue. A similarly pointed example comes at the end of the poem, when the epithet 'man-slaying' (*androphonos*), which is characteristic of Hector, is applied to Achilles at the moment Priam supplicates him for the return of his son's body: 'and he kissed the terrible, man-slaying hands, which had killed many of his sons' (24.478-9). Such deliberate and artful use of traditional language is characteristic of the *Iliad*.

The terms 'formula' or 'formulaic', then, should not be taken to imply something dull and mechanical. No doubt in the hands of inferior bards the formular style led to predictable and pedestrian poetry, where the singer struggled to use the epic diction creatively. In Homer, by contrast, we have a poet who is in complete control of his story and his characters and able to adapt traditional epic language to express exactly what he wants to say. With such a poet there is no conflict between tradition and innovation; on the contrary, it is the traditional style which makes his individual creativity possible in the first place. Moreover, as the noun-epithet system makes clear, the poet can create various effects through his skilled use of repetition, and this principle (repetition with variation) is in fact the basic building-block of Homer's oral traditional style as a whole, which he uses to generate structure and meaning at every level. We see this process at its best in the poet's deployment of traditional story patterns and typical scenes, to which we will now turn.

Just as formulas are based on verbal repetition, so story patterns and typical scenes are dependent on repeated situations and events. Thus, for example, the story pattern of 'the abducted woman' (Helen, Chryseis, Briseis) underlies both the origins of the war and the initial quarrel of the *Iliad*. Similarly, the story pattern of 'the angry hero's withdrawal' is applied not only to Achilles to generate the larger plot, but also to Paris (6.325-36), Aeneas (13.459-61), and Meleager (9.524-99). The last example, spoken by Phoenix to Achilles, is particularly striking, not only for the parallels drawn between Meleager and Achilles (will Achilles make the same mistake as Meleager by refusing to return to battle at the right time, i.e. when gifts are offered?), but also because Phoenix identifies the tale of Meleager as a traditional story that Achilles should learn from (9.524-6):

'This is what we have heard in the glorious tales
of past heroes too, when furious anger came upon one of them:
that they might be won over by gifts and talked round with words.'

Like the poet himself, Phoenix is here using a traditional narrative pattern and the audience's familiarity with it to make his point – but one that Achilles chooses disastrously to ignore.

As with such story patterns, we see in the poet's deployment of typical scenes both his and his audience's expertise in what we might call the grammar of epic. It had long been known that Homeric narrative describes the same action (for example, bathing, eating, sacrificing, receiving a guest, sleeping, launching and beaching a ship, deliberating in assembly, taking an oath, donning armour, fighting, dying, lamenting, and so on) in similar ways and in various levels of detail, but only in the 1930s did

Walter Arend show how integral these 'typical scenes' were to the poet's compositional technique. He demonstrated how each of them could be expanded or contracted to suit the needs of their context, creating a great variety of effects. Thus sacrifice scenes alone can be divided into twenty-one separate elements, with no two sacrifice scenes being the same, and such variety is found in every kind of typical scene. To see the structural flexibility of this technique and its effect on meaning, it is best to consider some examples, so let us start with the poem's four major arming scenes: Paris (3.328-38), Agamemnon (11.16-46), Patroclus (16.130-44), and Achilles (19.364-91).

Each of these follows the same basic sequence (first greaves, followed by breastplate, sword, shield, helmet, and finally spear), but there are meaningful differences between them. As Paris prepares for his duel with Menelaus, we are told that his breastplate was not his but had to be borrowed from his brother Lycaon, underlining the fact that Paris usually fights from afar with his bow, and so will be no match for his battle-hardened opponent. Agamemnon's breastplate and sword are richly decorated with precious materials (gold, silver, blue enamel), stressing his wealth and power as commander of the Achaeans, but also his vanity, while his shield, crowned with figures (Gorgo, Terror, Panic) elsewhere found on the aegis of Athena (5.738-42), heralds his initial success in the fighting, but also emphasizes his tendency to bluster (he is soon wounded and forced to retreat). When Patroclus dons Achilles' armour, he is unable to carry Achilles' massive spear (no other Achaean can), and thus the poet underlines the fact that, despite his attempt to play the surrogate, Patroclus is no Achilles. Finally, Achilles' arming scene, the most important in the poem, has already been prefaced by the detailed description of his shield's manufacture by Hephaestus in the previous book (18.478-608), so rather than dwell again on the shield's decoration, the poet emphasizes its gleaming with a simile (it is like a fire on land which is out of reach of sailors caught in a storm), and inserts an element unattested elsewhere (Achilles checking the armour to see if it fits him) in order to foreground Achilles' unique position as the recipient of new armour made by a god. The concluding reference to the spear repeats the story of its origins already given in Patroclus' arming scene (it was a gift from the centaur Cheiron to Achilles' father, Peleus), stressing Achilles' right to wield the weapon and his ability to succeed where Patroclus failed.

Three of these four arming scenes (Paris excepted) are preludes to the hero's *aristeia* ('best moment'), a term used to describe the point in the fighting where the hero sweeps all before him. And in each of the poem's five major *aristeia* (Diomedes in Books 5-6, Agamemnon in 11, Hector in 15-16, Patroclus in 16, Achilles in 19-22) we see a similarly deliberate variation in detail to suit the context. Diomedes, for example, does not strip his enemy's corpse but is given golden armour in exchange for bronze by Glaucus, a symbol of his irresistibility in battle. Hector's glory in killing Patroclus is undercut by the fact that Patroclus has already been dazed and wounded by others (Apollo and Euphorbus): as Patroclus reminds the boasting Hector, 'you are the third to slay me' (16.850). As the central hero of the *Iliad*, Achilles is given an especially elaborate *aristeia*, which includes his being attacked by a god (the river Xanthos), while the struggle over his victim's corpse is expanded into the great encounter with Priam that ends the poem.

Arming scenes and *aristeia* are subsets of the larger cluster of typical motifs that make up battle narrative as a whole, which is such a large and fundamental part of the poem. Homer surveys all the stages of combat, from the first preparations for fighting to the recovery and burial of the dead. And here too, despite the repeated narrative patterns, there is no one battle scene the same as any other, and the poet creates meaning by variation on the underlying motifs. The poet's vision is strikingly cinematic, as he moves the focus from the widescreen scenes of mass fighting – where 'shield pressed on shield, helmet on helmet, man on man' (13.131) – to the individual duels. The fighting is stylized to an extent: it is much more decisive than actual warfare, since the warrior is killed or rescued and there are no walking wounded, and the lengthy passages of flyting (the exchange of abusive speeches before duels) are the stuff of poetry, but much would be familiar to an archaic-period audience from their own experience of battle. Aside from repetition, one of the basic principles of Homeric style is amplification: in other words, the more important an action or character is, the more elaborated the typical scene becomes, and thus, for example, more space is given to the fighting and deaths of major heroes like Sarpedon, Patroclus, and Hector than to any of the other 240 named warriors killed in the *Iliad*.

One of the most characteristic elements of Homer's style is the use of similes. Short similes of the type 'the hero roared like a lion' are common in ancient Near Eastern literature (including the Old Testament), but the long or extended simile which develops the comparison over many verses is unique to Homeric epic and much imitated by later epic poets (notably Apollonius and Virgil). There are approximately 1128 lines of simile in the *Iliad* (7.2% of its 15693 verses) which comprise some 153 short and 197 long similes. The figures for the *Odyssey* (87 short and only 45 long similes) show that the *Iliad* uses four times as many extended similes. This does not prove separate authorship of the two poems, but it does point to their different settings: the *Iliad* is much more concentrated on a particular location and time than is the *Odyssey*, and the *Iliad*'s extended similes help set the action of the poem within the wider world, as can be seen from the similes' most popular subjects (weather and nature, hunting and herding, human technology). More than three-quarters of the *Iliad*'s extended similes occur in battle scenes, but one should beware the common idea that they serve to provide 'relief' from the monotony of fighting, since most of the similes depict turbulence, hostility, and suffering of various kinds and thus intensify (rather than negate) the force and violence of the narrative. Similes have a variety of functions, but one of the most basic is to focus the audience's attention on a particular person, and their frequency in the battle scenes is one way in which the poet individualizes the deaths of the warriors, whether they are major heroes or rank-and-file fighters.

Short similes can in themselves be highly effective, as in the description of Apollo's attack on the Achaean camp: 'and his coming was like nightfall' (1.47). But the principle of amplification (discussed above) means that important moments are generally marked by longer or by multiple similes. Thus Achilles' return to the fighting is heralded by the longest lion simile in the poem (20.164-73), while an accumulation of five extended similes marks the introduction of the Achaean forces (2.455-83) and the fierce battle to recover Patroclus' body (17.725-59). Similes often foreshadow what is to come in the narrative: for example, when Achilles likens himself and Patroclus to a mother and a crying girl, the parental imagery foreshadows his intense grief at Patroclus' death (16.7-11); similarly, when Achilles grieves for Patroclus like a father wailing for his dead son (23.222-5), this prepares for the importance of his own father Peleus' grief in the compassion he will show to Priam, another bereft father. Similes can also express the viewpoint of a particular character, as when Priam sees the advancing Achilles as the baleful star known as Orion's Dog: 'it is the brightest star, but a sign of suffering, bringing much fever for wretched mortals' (22.30-1).

The most popular subjects (e.g. lions, boars, birds, cattle, weather, fire) are likely to be traditional, whereas the unique ones, which are often the most memorable, will have been composed for their specific context. Thus, for example, the moment when Athena saves Menelaus from Pandarus' truce-breaking arrow is marked by two unique similes: Athena deflects the missile 'like a mother brushing a fly from her child as he lies sweetly sleeping' (4.130-1), and blood covers Menelaus' wound 'as when a woman stains ivory with crimson dye, a Maionian or Carian woman, to make a cheek-piece for horses' (4.141-2). The contrast between human effort and divine ease evident in Athena's protection of Menelaus is also seen in the simile that compares Apollo's destruction of the Achaean wall to a little boy's demolition of sand-castles on the sea-shore (15.363-6):

He builds them up as playthings in his childish way,
and then delights in flattening them with hands and feet.
So did you, lord Apollo, flatten all the work and toil
of the Argives, and stirred up panic among them.

Like multiple similes, these unique images draw the audience's attention to crucial phases in the narrative, as when Menelaus relents in his quarrel with Antilochus and so avoids the kind of disastrous conflict that Agamemnon had started in Book 1 (23.597-9):

And Menelaus' heart
was melted, like the dew on the ears of ripening corn,
when the ploughlands are bristling with the crop.

Finally, extended similes do not simply liken one thing to another but create multiple points of comparison, whose effect is a deepening and complex resonance: so, for example, when Priam enters Achilles' hut, he is compared to an exiled murderer who is seeking asylum at a rich man's house in another land and whose arrival causes amazement (24.480-4). The comparison is arresting in its detail and seeming inappropriateness, but the audience will recall that the theme of the fleeing migrant is also attached to two of Achilles' closest comrades, Phoenix (9.478-84) and Patroclus, and that Patroclus was forced to leave his native city because of an involuntary murder (23.85-90). So Priam is likened to two men who found succour and protection in the house of Achilles' father, which encourages the audience to wonder whether the helpless Priam will fare as well now that Achilles is in charge.

Like similes, metaphors create analogies between separate things, but do so in a more compressed, and potentially more arresting, manner. The metaphorical force even of formulaic expressions such as 'winged words' and 'shepherd of the people' is not completely dulled by repetition: they mark the 'words' as impressive and reinforce the leader's obligation to act in the best interests of his followers. But more striking are the metaphors which blend ideas in unexpected ways, such as when Hector speaks of the Trojans giving Paris 'a coat of stones' (3.57) for all the harm he has caused them, or when Heracles is said to have 'widowed the streets' of Troy in revenge for the treachery of Laomedon (5.642). As with similes, metaphors are frequently used in battle scenes to make the action more vivid: weapons are 'eager to glut themselves with flesh' (e.g. 11.574), a dead warrior 'slept the sleep of bronze' (11.241), and when the Achaeans return to battle, 'all the earth around them laughed at the flashing bronze' (19.362-3).

Perhaps the most striking feature of Homeric style (apart from its use of formulas) is the great preponderance of direct speech. As Aristotle observed (*Poetics* ch. 24):

> Homer deserves praise for many other attributes, but especially for his grasp – unique among epic poets – of his role as a poet. For the poet should say as little as possible in his own voice, since that is not *mimesis* ('imitation'). Other epic poets act in their own voice throughout, and engage in *mimesis* briefly and infrequently. But Homer, with little prelude, immediately 'brings on stage' a man, woman or some other figure, and they are all fully characterized.

The theatrical term 'brings on stage' emphasizes Homer's proto-dramatic quality, which is a consequence (as Aristotle explains) of the high proportion of character speech: 45% of the *Iliad* is direct speech (the *Odyssey* is even higher at 68%, since Odysseus himself narrates Books 9-12), and speeches are integral to many of the most important episodes in the poem: for example, the quarrel in Book 1, Hector and his family (Book 6), the embassy to Achilles (9), Hector and the dying Patroclus (16), Achilles and the dying Hector (22), Achilles' meeting with Priam (24). Being a good speaker is in itself part of the heroic ideal: Achilles' old tutor Phoenix recalls how he was sent by Peleus to ensure that this son became 'both a speaker of words and a doer of deeds' (9.443), and it is no coincidence that the major heroes of the Homeric epics (Achilles and Odysseus) are also the most eloquent (note the Trojan Antenor's praise of Odysseus' skill as a speaker at 3.216-24).

The style and vocabulary of the speeches are different from the narrative. They are more personal in the sense of being more emotional and rhetorical, and they use more superlatives, negatives, and value judgements: thus the word *schetlios* ('cruel') occurs 29 times in character speech but only once in the narrator's voice, *hubris* ('insult') 26 times to 3, *aidôs* ('shame') 24 times to 1, and so on. Moreover, the different styles and content of particular speeches also serve to characterize the individual heroes. Thus, for example, each of the three figures who undertake the embassy in Book 9 delivers a speech to match his character: Odysseus is rational and calculating, Phoenix affectionate and didactic, Ajax blunt and bewildered by Achilles' complexity. Achilles has the most individual style of all, and his speeches in rejection of the embassy display his character to the full, using violent and abusive language, exaggeration, simile, and *hapax legomena* (words used only once in the poem (80 in total); he also uses the most words (18) that do not occur anywhere else in Greek) in order to articulate his idiosyncratic view of his situation.

Finally, let us consider the structure of the poem. The division into 24 books is not original but was probably introduced by Alexandrian scholars in the third century BC, each book numbered with a letter of the Greek alphabet (their lengths vary from 424 verses in Book 19 to 909 in Book 5). Before that authors refer only to distinct episodes such as 'the *aristeia* of Diomedes' (Herodotus 2.116) or 'the Catalogue of Ships' (Thucydides 1.10.4). The Alexandrian book divisions occasionally coincide with particular episodes (e.g. the quarrel in Book 1, the embassy in 9, the meeting of Achilles and Priam in 24), but often they simply interrupt them, as with Diomedes' *aristeia* which continues from Book 5 into 6. Despite its great size, the *Iliad* covers only a short period in the Trojan War, concentrating on just four days of fighting from the tenth year (2.1-23.108), flanked by scenes which depict the cause and resolution of Achilles' anger (Books 1 and 24). As Aristotle again observed, Homer did not make the same mistake as the later poets of the Epic Cycle, who tried to cover everything from start to finish, leading merely to a dull sequence of events (*Poetics* ch. 23); rather he chose a single, unified action within the story of Troy's fall (the anger of Achilles) and expanded it in a way that allows his narrative to embrace the entire war.

Thus the poem includes events which would be more appropriate at the start of the war: the catalogue of ships in Book 2, the duel between Paris and Menelaus and Helen's review of the major Achaean heroes for Priam in Book 3, the building of the Achaean defensive wall and ditch in Book 7. But each of these 'logically' earlier episodes is also adapted to its place within the *Iliad*: the catalogue heralds the scale and importance of the ensuing battle, the duel (and Paris' unmerited escape) reinforces the original Trojan crime, while the Achaean defences underline their vulnerability to Trojan attack once Achilles has withdrawn. And as well as evoking events earlier in the war, the poem also foreshadows the death of Achilles (e.g. 18.95-101) and the fall of Troy (12.10-35). The closing lines of the *Iliad* look forward to the continuing warfare, as the Trojans post look-outs during Hector's funeral in case the Achaeans spring an early attack (24.799-800), and the poem thus draws attention to the fact that its end is not an end, and that it is part of a wider epic tradition.

The creative use of time (past and future) is therefore one of the best examples of the *Iliad*'s careful and sophisticated structure, which in turn is one of the clearest proofs of the single creative intelligence behind the work as a whole. And just as the poem's deliberate planning is evident in its unity of theme (namely, the cause and consequences of Achilles' anger), so it also emerges in the long-range preparation of future developments in the narrative: for example, Zeus saves Sarpedon 'for the time being' (5.662) in preparation for his later killing by Patroclus in Book 16, and Patroclus' own death soon after is already prophesied by Zeus in Books 8 and 15 (8.470-7, 15.59-71). Such clear prophecies do not remove interest: on the contrary, the audience's knowledge of the outcome creates its own suspense, as they wonder *how* the poet will take them there.

It was noted above that repetition is a fundamental principle of Homeric poetry and this is equally true of its structure, as the number of similar scenes and the frequency of ring-composition show. There are, for example, a large number of correspondences between the deaths of Sarpedon, Patroclus, and Hector, the only heroes who are given death speeches; indeed, the same four lines are used to describe the deaths of Patroclus and Hector (16.855-8 = 22.361-4), each of whom prophesies his killer's death, so that the connections between the scenes prepare for the death of Achilles himself. Ring-composition is a basic technique for articulating structure in ancient Greek literature (especially for marking the end of works) and it is used nowhere more impressively than in the *Iliad*. Thus in both Book 1 and 24 an old man (Chryses/Priam) supplicates an Achaean hero and offers a ransom for the release of his child; in both books Thetis travels to Olympus on behalf of her son; Apollo also plays a crucial role, inflicting the plague on the Achaeans in Book 1 for ignoring the ransom offered for Chryseis and haranguing the gods in Book 24 so that they will support the ransoming of Hector's corpse; and there is even an identical period of 22 days covered in each (plague and divine holiday in 1, mutilation and burial in 24). Further parallels could be added, but the important point is not mere echoing: for whereas Chryses fails in his appeal, Priam succeeds in his, creating a powerful and satisfying sense of resolution and closure.

In conclusion, we have seen how the basic features of oral-derived poetry (from noun-epithet systems to repeated story patterns and typical scenes) make it possible for Homer to generate his song and to create meaning within it. It is important that we try to understand these traditional techniques, since they show the extent to which Homer was a master of his tradition and a uniquely gifted poet.

Chapter 3

The Hero and Homeric Society

Despite their desire 'always to be the best and to excel above others' – so Hippolochus' injunction to Glaucus (6.208) and Peleus' to Achilles (11.784) – the Iliadic heroes are not rampant individualists, but fundamentally social heroes; that is, they exist as part of a wider society whose estimation of them is central to their heroic identity. This chapter will examine the communal basis of heroism, showing how a hero's ability to balance personal concerns (ambitions, grievances, etc.) with the good of his community is key to the portrayal of the work's central figures. As we shall see, the suffering and disorder depicted in the *Iliad* stem not from any fundamental failure in Homeric society or ethics *per se*, but from the character, emotions, and errors of the heroes themselves, and especially from their attempts to put personal claims to honour above the interests of their community.

First, it is important that the word 'hero' itself be understood correctly. Nowadays we reserve the term for people who have done something unambiguously positive: for example, firemen who rush into a burning building to save people, or soldiers who fight for their country and to protect their comrades. In ancient Greek culture, however, the 'heroes' are not simply positive figures. They are men from a distinct period before our own, the heroic age or 'race of men half-divine', as Homer calls them (12.23), who, far from being simply paragons of virtue, are characterized by their excessiveness, both for good and for ill. The heroic generation possesses greater vitality and strength than ours: the heroes are *megathumoi*, often translated as 'great-hearted', but literally meaning that they are full of *thumos*, the spirit of life. One of the key words for this energy or force is *menos* ('strength'), which can propel the heroes to acts of superhuman and admirable prowess. Yet their heroic power is double-edged, because it can also lead to less desirable qualities: excessive anger, violence, cruelty, pride, recklessness, and egotism. So there is a tension within heroism itself in that the very energy which makes the heroes outstanding is also the source of their instability and danger (both to themselves and to others). The *Iliad*, then, is a sophisticated epic, which not only celebrates the heroic world but also explores the nature of heroism itself.

Heroes, it should also be stressed, come in a variety of forms: Achilles is not the same as Odysseus, nor Ajax the same as Hector (let alone Paris). In other words, the basic drive 'always to be the best' does not lead to a series of identical heroic characters. Diomedes, for example, acts as a foil for Achilles in the first half of the poem, since he is able to excuse Agamemnon's insults in a way that Achilles could not (4.364-418), highlighting the latter's anger and resentment. (It is equally true, however, that well-balanced characters like Diomedes are less dramatic and interesting than excessive ones like Achilles.) Even if we sum up the heroic ideal in terms of being outstanding as 'both a speaker of words and a doer of deeds' (9.443), each hero will possess these abilities in his own individual way. Thus Odysseus and Nestor excel as speakers, Achilles and Ajax as fighters. To us such a close connection between fighting well and speaking well seems odd, but from a Homeric perspective they complement one another perfectly, since the battlefield and the assembly (*agorê*) are the foremost arenas in which the hero can excel and thereby benefit both himself and his community. Moreover, as the lowly Thersites discovers to his cost, one may acquire respect through speaking but one also needs some status to speak in the first place: for despite voicing much the same criticisms of Agamemnon as Achilles had done in Book 1, Thersites lacks the status to express them and is beaten by Odysseus, whose action is applauded by the Achaean army (2.211-77).

Yet, for all their variety, the Homeric heroes are united by their focus on the pursuit of honour (*timê*), which is the bedrock of the heroic world and its values. *Timê* denotes the way one is valued in the eyes of others and the esteem which they confer. A wide range of qualities create honour (e.g. age, noble birth), but foremost in the *Iliad* are one's status within the community and one's prowess in battle, since these lie at the heart of the tension between Agamemnon and Achilles. Esteem is manifested in many different ways too, including grants of land, food, and wine (as described by Sarpedon to Glaucus (12.310-21): on this passage see further below), and in the form of booty or war-prizes (*gera*) granted to the foremost warriors: one such prize (Briseis) is the origin of Achilles' quarrel with Agamemnon. All Homeric heroes, not just Achilles, are driven by their concern for *timê*. However, since honour is conferred by others, and since it depends on a complex and subjective interplay of power, status, and one's evaluation of other people, it is something that has to be carefully managed and negotiated (something the heavy-handed Agamemnon is unable to do), and problems can arise (as with Achilles) if an individual feels he is being short-changed for his efforts, or as Achilles puts it, when 'coward and brave are held in equal honour' (9.319).

Apart from *timê*, two other concepts are central to a proper understanding of Homeric heroism, namely *aidôs* ('shame', 'respect') and *kleos* ('fame', 'reputation'). Having a sense of shame (*aidôs*) prevents an individual from doing disgraceful actions (e.g. retreating in battle) that provoke indignation (*nemesis*) in others. More positively, *aidôs* also expresses an individual's 'respect' for others, and the need to take their separate claim to honour into account. In other words, the importance of *aidôs* shows that the heroic drive 'always to be the best and to excel above others' is not a manifesto for pure self-interest, since success relies on respecting as well as being respected by others. A hero's concern for how he is spoken of (his *kleos*), both during his lifetime and after his death, is an extension of his concern for his honour. It is a basic tenet of Homeric heroism that the fame of great achievements offers a kind of immortality, so that Hector goes to face Achilles determined either to win or to die with glorious *kleos*: 'May I not die without a fight and ingloriously (*akleiôs*), but having done some great deed for men of the future to hear of' (22.304-5). The fact that death is absolute in the *Iliad*, with no possibility of immortality (as in the *Odyssey*, Hesiod, and the Epic Cycle), gives a particular urgency to the hero's desire for honour in his lifetime, especially when (as with Achilles: 9.410-16) he has given up the chance of a long life in order to face certain death at Troy.

People often speak of a 'heroic code' operating in the *Iliad*, but the term is misleading and best avoided, since it suggests a kind of 'highway code' for heroes, a rule book they can look up, which will tell them what they should do in a particular situation. Heroism, however, is not so inflexible; on the contrary, it is embodied in human beings with powerful emotions and competing obligations, so that what the hero chooses to do (and what it is appropriate for him to do) will depend on a variety of factors, including his character and particular circumstances. Nonetheless, the *Iliad* does endorse some basic principles of human interaction, which are far from being selfish and individualistic. As we shall see, the errors made by Agamemnon, Achilles, and Hector show the need to avoid pushing one's own claim to *timê* too far, lest it damage both the agent himself and his community. Once again, self-interest has to be balanced with regard for others. This is well illustrated by the quarrel between Menelaus and Antilochus in Book 23, which replays many of the tensions inherent in the quarrel between Achilles and Agamemnon in Book 1, but with a less disastrous outcome. Both men declare their right to the same prize (*geras*), this time a horse won in a chariot race rather than a woman won in war, but both also realize that other factors override their claim to the prize: Antilochus (unlike Achilles) respects Menelaus' superior status, while Menelaus (unlike Agamemnon) recognizes that he owes much to his opponent, who is fighting on his behalf (23.586-611). Neither man allows his desire for honour to go too far, and a potentially disastrous conflict is averted.

The communal basis of heroism emerges clearly from a consideration of Homeric society and the structures of authority within it. Although Homeric society is (like Homeric language) a poetic composite with details drawn from different historical periods (including a certain nostalgia for the grand old world of Mycenaean 'lords of men'), it is nonetheless a coherent and credible world. Moreover, since oral poetry must constantly develop in order to address the changing concerns of its audience or risk becoming irrelevant and obsolete, the fictional society of the *Iliad* must engage with the fundamental moral and political concerns of its audience. The *Iliad* does so by avoiding a narrow ideological stance (for example, by being pro- or anti-monarchy or aristocracy), but instead explores broad themes which are as relevant today as they were in Homer's time, none more so perhaps than the relationship between the leader and his community. The question of how a leader should behave in order to ensure the well-being of his people is one that is posed on both the Achaean and the Trojan side. For, as we shall see, not only Agamemnon and Achilles, but also Paris, Hector, and Priam make mistakes which damage or destroy their communities.

The symbiosis of leader and led pervades the poem. Both the Achaeans and the Trojans hold assemblies, where the decisions of the army's or community's leaders are ratified by the rank-and-file (e.g. 1.54-305, 7.345-79). Moreover, the poem's clearest statement of what it is to be a hero, in a speech delivered by Sarpedon (a Lycian ally of the Trojans) to his comrade Glaucus, focuses on the relationship between the hero and his people (12.310-21)

> 'Glaucus, why are we two most held in honour
> with the best seats and cuts of meat and full cups
> in Lycia, and all look on us like gods?
> And we enjoy a large estate by the banks of the Xanthos,
> fine land for orchards and wheat-bearing ploughland.
> That is why we must take our stand in the first rank of the Lycians
> and face the raging heat of battle,
> so that among the close-armoured Lycians people may say:
> "Not without glory are those who rule in Lycia,
> our leaders, who consume fattened sheep

and choice honey-sweet wine; but they have strength
and courage too, it seems, since they fight in the first ranks of the
    Lycians." '

The people grant the hero high status and material honours in return for
his acceptance of the responsibility to protect them. This reciprocity
works because both parties benefit from the relationship. Significantly,
where heroes in the *Iliad* forget they are fighting for the people (as much
as for themselves) and allow their personal concerns to damage the
well-being of the community, disgrace and disaster ensue. Paris, for
example, does not care what the Trojans or their allies think of him – 'he
was hated by them all like black death' (3.454) – and refuses to give Helen
back, for purely selfish reasons, when to do so risks destroying his
community (7.345-64).

The social formation of heroism, then, is seen in the conduct of all the
major figures on both sides, especially Agamemnon, Achilles, and Hector.
Let us first consider the portrayal of Hector before looking at the Achaean
heroes. Hector is presented as particularly concerned with what other
people think, and he uses the idea of imaginary third-person speech
('someone will say …') much more often than any other hero (e.g.
6.459-62, 479-81, 7.87-91). However, Hector's fear of disgrace in the
eyes of others turns out to be one of the main factors in his death, and
Andromache's prediction 'your own might (*menos*) will destroy you'
(6.407) proves true. For after rejecting Polydamas' 'good advice' (as the
narrator calls it, 18.313) to shelter within the walls of Troy, Hector, carried
away by his recent success in reaching the Achaean ships and killing
Patroclus, orders the Trojans to stay out on the plain overnight, and so
enables Achilles to inflict huge losses on them when he returns to the
fighting. Hector's awareness of his mistake and the damage his desire for
glory has done to his people crucially influences his decision to reject the
anguished appeals of his parents and stay to face Achilles (22.98-110):

Then, greatly troubled, he spoke to his own proud heart:
'What am I to do? If I go back inside the gates and walls,
Polydamas will be the first to lay reproaches on me,
for he urged me to lead the Trojans back into the city
during this last fatal night, when godlike Achilles was roused.
But I did not listen to him – it would have been far better if I had.
So now that I have ruined my people by my own reckless folly,
I feel shame before the Trojan men and the Trojan women with their
    trailing robes,

in case someone who is less of a man than I may say:
"Hector trusted in his own might and ruined his people."
So they will say; and then it would be far better for me
to go face to face with Achilles and kill him and return home,
or else die gloriously myself in front of the city.'

Hector knows he has failed in his duty of care for his people, and the shame this entails drives him to face Achilles in the hope of winning his honour back either by victory or a glorious death. Yet Hector's death will be even more ruinous for the Trojans, and so there is a terrible irony in Hector's reaction to his dilemma, for the very qualities which make him such a great hero (his sense of shame and his pride in his status and abilities) lead him to make a decision which will doom not only himself but also his family and his city. Homer has deliberately portrayed Hector as the family and community oriented hero *par excellence* (especially in Book 6, where Hector returns to Troy) in order to underline the difficulty of his final choice, as he puts one aspect of heroism (his honour) above another (protection of his people). However, Hector's conflict does not mean that heroism itself is self-contradictory or doomed to failure. Rather it shows that in the absence of a simple 'heroic code' that spells out which aspect of heroism should win out in any given situation, it is up to the individual hero to balance the competing obligations that come with his status. In Hector we see one man's perspective on the tension within heroism between self-assertion and concern for others. Hector's decision, awesome yet fatal, to put his personal quest for honour above all other considerations illuminates the difficulty and complexity of heroism itself.

As with Hector, Agamemnon's and Achilles' portrayal throughout the poem explores the potential conflict within heroism between individual ambition and collective good, and the dangers of putting personal honour above all else. The poem begins with Agamemnon rejecting the unanimous will of the Achaean army, who approve Chryses' offer of a ransom for his captured daughter (1.22-5). When Apollo's plague strikes the Achaeans as a result, Agamemnon is forced to return his prize (Chryseis), without gaining the ransom. Agamemnon grudgingly gives up Chryseis because (as he says) 'I want the people to survive rather than to perish' (1.117), but no sooner is this crisis averted than Agamemnon sparks another one, for he demands a replacement prize, even though all the booty has already been divided among the Achaean leaders. Achilles urges Agamemnon to take a longer view of the matter, as a good leader would: 'we Achaeans will compensate you three and four times over, if ever Zeus grants that we tear apart the well-walled city of Troy' (1.127-9).

Agamemnon, however, puts the *immediate* replenishment of his *timê* above everything else, with disastrous results for himself and the army.

The quarrel escalates between the two Achaean leaders in a vivid series of angry speeches, which brilliantly express the sensitivities of each man. Accusations of 'you *always* do x' and 'you *never* do y' are exchanged: thus, for example, Achilles complains 'I never receive a prize equal to yours' (1.163), while Agamemnon retorts 'strife and war and battles are always dear to you' (1.177). This kind of talk, so typical of angry arguments, also creates the sense of a long-standing tension between the two men, as if this is not the first time they have clashed. When Achilles criticizes Agamemnon's demand for a replacement prize, tactlessly addressing him as 'most glorious son of Atreus, most rapacious of all men' (1.122), Agamemnon is unable to cope with the public challenge to his authority, and so issues a counter-challenge to Achilles, insisting that he will take away Achilles' prize (Briseis), 'so that you may know well how much more powerful I am than you' (1.185-6). Agamemnon feels himself backed into a corner by Achilles and lacks the diplomatic skills (of an Odysseus, for example) necessary to defuse the situation; instead he falls back on his status and rank, where he knows he is superior to Achilles, and insists on an immediate manifestation of his *timê* (Briseis), even at the risk of alienating his best fighter.

The errors made by both Agamemnon and Achilles are clearly expressed in Nestor's advice to them (1.275-84):

'You, great man though you are, do not take the girl from this man,
but let her be, since the sons of the Achaeans first gave her to him as
     a prize.
And you, son of Peleus, do not seek to strive with a king
by force, since a sceptred king to whom Zeus grants glory
has a greater portion of honour.
You may be stronger and have a goddess for your mother,
but he is greater, because he rules over more people.
Son of Atreus, bring your rage to an end; I beg you
to let go your anger against Achilles, who is a mighty
bulwark for all the Achaeans against the evils of war.'

Nestor rebukes both men, Agamemnon for undoing the original distribution of prizes and neglecting Achilles' importance to the campaign, and Achilles for quarrelling with his superior. He urges them to respect the other man's particular excellence and claim to honour, Achilles' prowess and Agamemnon's rank. Nestor does not place one claim to *timê* above the other, but insists instead that both deserve respect and both are crucial to the collective good: Agamemnon must recognize that 'the sons of the Achaeans' gave Briseis to Achilles as a communal recognition of his efforts and value to the mission, while Achilles must cease from publicly challenging Agamemnon and thereby threatening the hierarchy and order of the Achaean army. As Nestor points out, their quarrel benefits only the Trojans (1.255-8). Both heroes, however, ignore Nestor's advice: Agamemnon says he agrees with Nestor, but instead of taking back his demand for Briseis he continues to insist on his status, accusing Achilles of wanting to be supreme commander (1.286-9), while Achilles claims that to submit to Agamemnon would make him 'a coward and a nobody' (1.293). Each hero fails in his obligation to his community: Agamemnon alienates his best fighter and damages the expedition, while Achilles not only knows that his withdrawal from battle will doom many of his comrades (1.240-4), but is prepared to use their deaths to force Agamemnon to make good his loss of honour (1.408-12).

Both men are also to blame for the failure of the embassy in Book 9. Agamemnon's offer of material compensation comes with no apology to Achilles or any expression of gratitude for his efforts or acknowledgement of his worth. Achilles, on the other hand, fails to accept that there are other factors, especially his ties to his fellow Achaeans, which might (and should) cancel out the perceived shortcomings in Agamemnon's offer, and he allows his anger to blind him to all other concerns, so that he rejects the socially approved process of compensation. Unlike Book 1, however, where Agamemnon started the crisis and we are led to sympathize with Achilles, Book 9 shows Achilles to be no less intransigent and unreasonable in his demand for honour, and equally culpable for damaging the Achaean army.

Nestor advises Agamemnon to appeal to Achilles 'with soothing gifts and flattering words' (9.113), but the gifts and words deployed by Agamemnon are problematic. First, Agamemnon engages in competitive largesse, offering gifts on such a magnificent scale as to underline his superiority to Achilles (9.121-56); secondly, far from going to Achilles in person or expressing himself in flattering terms, Agamemnon sends a message which culminates in a renewed demand that Achilles recognize his superiority (9.160-1):

'And let him take his place below me, since I am the more kingly and can claim to be his senior by birth.'

Wisely, Odysseus omits these closing words when he relates

Agamemnon's speech to Achilles, but Achilles still senses the high-handed tone of Agamemnon's offer. Odysseus replaces the demand for submission with his own two-fold appeal (9.300-6): first, he entreats Achilles to pity his Achaean comrades, who are suffering in his absence – the appeal to pity is also used by the two other members of the embassy, Phoenix and Ajax (9.494-7, 628-32); and secondly, he entices Achilles with the prospect of great honour and glory if he returns to the fighting, especially if he kills Hector, who is now enjoying great success on the battlefield. Achilles, however, only recognizes, or relearns, the value of pity much later (when confronted by Priam in Book 24), while the appeal to honour rings hollow, since Achilles believes Agamemnon has undermined the entire system that generates and preserves honour in the first place.

It is sometimes said that Achilles is rejecting the 'heroic code' itself in his response to the embassy. However, what Achilles is criticizing is not heroism *per se*, but rather Agamemnon's perceived abuse of it (and his fellow Achaeans' collusion in that abuse). For it makes no sense to risk one's life for honour and glory, Achilles argues, if those rewards can be withheld or taken away, so that 'coward and brave are held in equal honour' (9.319). And the trade-off between the risk of death and the winning of honour is especially stark for Achilles because, as he reveals in his rejection of the embassy, he knows from his divine mother Thetis that, should he choose to stay and fight for glory at Troy, he is doomed to an early death (9.410-13). Moreover, Achilles thinks there is no guarantee that Agamemnon will not 'deceive' him or some other Achaean hero in this way again (9.344-5, 371-6). Yet, just as Agamemnon can be faulted for continuing to indulge his desire for dominance, so Achilles is being unreasonable in his reaction to Agamemnon's offer. For not only does Achilles put an infinite value on his damaged honour (no amount of gifts will satisfy him, he says (9.379-87), a position that is socially unacceptable and baffling to all the other Achaeans), but he also tries to replace the established protocols of compensation with a much more personal and incalculable demand, saying that he will not change his mind and return to battle 'until he [Agamemnon] has paid me back for all this heart-rending outrage' (9.387).

In other words, Achilles points to his *feelings* and Agamemnon's failure to assuage them – note his later wish that Agamemnon 'would treat me kindly' (16.72-3). But feelings are hard to account for within the formal system of compensation, and Achilles' inability to get over his anger at the original offence strikes all the other Achaeans as perverse; as Phoenix succinctly puts it, '*before now* your anger could not be blamed'

(9.523, emphasis added). And when Ajax points out that the anger even of a murdered man's relatives is restrained by accepting compensation from the killer (9.632-6), the excessiveness and selfishness of Achilles' continuing rage and refusal to accept the compensation are powerfully underlined. Achilles recognizes the disastrous consequences of his anger only when it is too late and Patroclus is dead: 18.107-11. To sum up, the problems with Agamemnon's offer (its competitiveness and superior tone) encourage us to understand what still rankles with Achilles; nonetheless, all the other Achaeans believe Achilles should get over his anger and hurt feelings – note especially Diomedes' condemnation of his 'arrogance' (9.699-700). Insofar, then, as a hero is measured by his success in balancing self-assertion against concern for others, Achilles' rejection of Agamemnon's offer and his comrades' advice is seen to be deeply anti-social. Moreover, it proves to be ultimately self-destructive.

Patroclus dies in an attempt to defend Achilles' honour (as well as to aid his fellow Achaeans), promising, as he goes into battle, that he will make Agamemnon regret his alienation of 'the best of the Achaeans' (16.269-74). Patroclus' death forces Achilles to recognize the duty that a hero owes his friends, and he regrets his excessive anger and egotism, albeit too late to save his closest friend (18.98-111). Blaming himself for his role in Patroclus' death, Achilles cares now only for the honour that will come from avenging that death. Though Achilles accepts Agamemnon's gifts in Book 19 and their reconciliation is publicly formalized, it is clear that the gifts mean nothing to him ('give them or keep them, I don't care' is his startling attitude: 19.145-8) and that his entire sense of honour is now invested in vengeance. Indeed, when Thetis reveals that Achilles is doomed to die soon after Hector, Achilles declares that he will pay any price to wipe out the shame of Patroclus' death: 'Then let me die immediately, since I was not to protect my comrade at his killing' (18.98-9). And just as Achilles moves the focus of his honour from rewards for valour to revenge, so he moves the target of his anger from Agamemnon to Hector.

Significantly, however, Achilles displays the same excessiveness and anger in his desire for revenge as he did in his desire to punish Agamemnon. Odysseus must insist on the needs of others (the soldiers need to eat before returning to battle), while Achilles can think only of killing Hector (19.148-72). But he does more than kill Hector, he mutilates his corpse (or at least attempts to, as the gods keep Hector's body fresh and unscathed: 23.184-91, 24.18-21, 410-23), dragging it behind his chariot (22.395-404). This is a shocking act, which violates a basic taboo protecting a dead man's body: though mutilation of a corpse is threatened elsewhere in the poem, Achilles is the only character to enact it. For while one may legitimately refuse to ransom a man (alive or dead), it is quite another thing to mutilate his corpse once the fighting is over, and Achilles' actions show that while he is right to avenge Hector's killing of Patroclus, he goes too far in his attempt to discharge his anger and alleviate his shame. Indeed, the *repeated* mutilation of Hector's body (which he continues for twelve days: 24.14-18, 31-2), and Achilles' inability to escape his grief and self-loathing despite this ultimate humiliation of his enemy, show that his approach to vengeance is self-defeating. By dehumanizing his enemy in this way (note that he also sacrifices twelve Trojan youths on the pyre of Patroclus: 18.336-7, 23.22-3, 181-2), Achilles merely extends his grief long after Patroclus has been buried and lamented, and compounds his inability to return to a balanced state of mind.

It takes the intervention of the gods to end Achilles' shameful disrespect of Hector's body, which Apollo criticizes as bestial and sub-human (24.40-5):

'His wits are out of joint and the mind
in his breast is unbending. His thoughts are savage like a lion's,
who gives in to his great strength and proud heart
and goes out to feast on the flocks that men keep.
Just so has Achilles murdered pity, and there is no shame in him,
shame that can both greatly harm and greatly benefit a man.'

The gods' pity leads to the meeting of Priam and Achilles and the ransoming of Hector's corpse, where Achilles regains the qualities of *eleos* ('pity') and *aidôs* ('shame', 'respect') which, the *Iliad* insists, are essential qualities of the man of honour. On Hermes' instructions, Priam appeals to Achilles in the name of his father Peleus, and as Achilles sees the grief and suffering of his own father mirrored in the Trojan king, the two men weep together (24.509-12):

So the two remembered, Priam crouched at Achilles' feet
and weeping loud for man-slaying Hector,
while Achilles wept for his own father, and then again
for Patroclus; and the sound of their groaning filled the hut.

In showing Priam the respect due to him (and, by extension, to Hector), Achilles emerges from his self-obsession and grief and recognizes the humanity of others. The key role played here by Achilles' ability to generalize moral values and show pity for shared human suffering suggests that Plato was right to call Homer the first and greatest of the tragic poets (e.g. *Republic* 595b, 607a). Indeed, Achilles not only pities Priam's suffering, but also tries to console him, telling of the two jars standing on Zeus' threshold, one dispensing evils and the other blessings: one can receive a mixture of good and evil, or undiluted evil, and so suffering is an inescapable part of being human (24.527-33). The only defence against suffering, Achilles explains, is endurance (24.549-51). Achilles here echoes the speech of Apollo at the start of Book 24, who complained of Achilles' inability to endure his grief for Patroclus in the right way (24.46-52). So, in urging Priam to mourn and move on, Achilles shows that he has not only recognized the universality of suffering, but has also learned from his own.

It would be a mistake, however, to see Achilles in Book 24 as having undergone a significant change of character. There are some remarkable differences, but the continuities are no less striking. Thus while he previously rejected the Achaean embassy and refused to give up his anger against Agamemnon, he now accepts Priam's supplication and relinquishes his fury against Hector. Yet despite his very different reaction, both anger and sensitivity to honour remain an essential part of Achilles' presentation. Achilles initially agrees to release Hector not out of selfless magnanimity, but because Thetis tells him that the gods, and especially Zeus, are angry with him and want him to accept Priam's ransom (24.133-40). Of course he still shows compassion for Priam, but his desire for *timê* remains fundamental (note how he placates the anger of Patroclus' ghost by saying that he too will share in the rich ransom: 24.591-5). Moreover, Achilles had treated the enemy kindly in the past, burying them with full honours, as he did for Andromache's father, Eëtion (6.416-20), or ransoming them (e.g. 21.34-46). So while it is true that Achilles' decision to accept Priam's ransom is a source of 'glory' (*kudos*), granted by Zeus (24.110), his reasons for doing so indicate not a change in character but a return to a more balanced state, as shown before his murderous rage against Hector set in, where respect is given to one's enemy. This idea of a return to a more normal life (and reintegration within the community) is underlined by Achilles once more eating and sleeping with a woman, as advised by his mother Thetis (24.128-31). For while he had previously refused to eat because of his grief for Patroclus and his rage to kill Hector (19.203-14), he now shares food with Priam and tells him the story of Niobe (who ate despite losing twelve children) to reinforce the idea that life must go on (24.601-20). And when Achilles and Priam go to sleep, Achilles goes to bed with Briseis, marking (via another ring-composition: see Chapter 2) the end of the poet's theme, Achilles' anger, which was sparked by Briseis' removal in Book 1 (24.675-6).

A similar combination of continuity and change is also seen in the portrayal of Achilles' anger itself. Achilles remains deeply sensitive to violations of his status, and so when Priam initially refuses to be seated (so eager is he to return to Troy with Hector's body: 24.552-8), Achilles takes this as a challenge to his authority, for the protocols of supplication (*hiketeia*) and hospitality (*xenia*) involved in their meeting mean that Achilles is very much in charge of the situation. Achilles angrily rebukes Priam and warns him that one more mistake will mean his death, even if he is a suppliant and supported by Zeus (24.568-70). At the same time, however, Achilles also shows an awareness of the potential negative consequences of his anger, and takes measures to guard against it. Thus he has Hector's body washed, anointed, and clothed in another room, in case Priam should see it and get angry, which might prompt Achilles to kill him (24.582-6). So Achilles is more aware of his anger, and able to avoid its disastrous consequences in a way impossible earlier in the poem, but his quick temper and readiness to react decisively in defence of his honour remain the same. Thus Book 24 does not present a new Achilles, but sets aspects of his character in a new context, where he is once again able to control his anger and show compassion. However, his less kind traits are still present; after all, the audience know that the war will continue and Achilles will kill more of Priam's sons (24.664-7).

In conclusion, the *Iliad* explores the complexity of heroism and shows the risks of putting personal claims to honour and pre-eminence before all else. In particular, the errors made by the poem's central figures, which lead to the destruction either of themselves or their people, show that concern for others is an essential part of heroism. The hero, if he is to flourish, must balance the pursuit of personal honour with the respect due to others and his obligations to the community as a whole. As we saw most clearly in Sarpedon's speech to Glaucus, a hero's honour depends crucially on his success in protecting his community. So although heroism relies on competitive masculinity, it is very far from being a form of selfish individualism. Finally, we may be far removed from the heroic age or Homer's own time, but we can still relate intimately and immediately to the *Iliad*'s depiction of heroism, since it presents human beings striving for recognition, and trying to understand their life, in relation to the demands of family, friends, and society as a whole.

Chapter 4
Mortals and Immortals

The gods' concern for mortals and their constant interference in human affairs is one of the most striking aspects of the poem (especially to a modern reader). This chapter will consider the gods both in their own right and in relation to humans, asking why the gods act as they do. It will also examine the gods' relationship to the fall of Troy, showing how the competing affections and plans of the various deities involved are subservient to the larger 'will of Zeus' (*Dios boulê*) which shapes the narrative of the poem. As we shall see, Homer's gods are not merely figures of literature, but an expression of a coherent theology. For the Homeric *kosmos* provides its audience with a compelling picture of the world, and of the ways in which gods and humans act and interact within it.

According to the historian Herodotus (2.53), writing in the fifth century BC, 'It was Homer and Hesiod who created for the Greeks a genealogy of the gods, gave the gods their names, assigned their honours and areas of expertise, and described their appearance.' Since there was no established church or priestly caste or sacred book to prescribe religious beliefs in ancient Greece, poets played a fundamental role in shaping religious ideas, and none more so than Homer, who was the foundation of all education, including what the Greeks thought about their gods. It is a measure of the spell of Homer that when the philosopher Xenophanes (who was active in the sixth century BC) wishes to criticize conventional religious belief, he attacks the theology of the great poets (fr. 11):

> Homer and Hesiod have attributed to the gods
> everything that men find shameful and blameworthy:
> stealing, adultery, and deceiving one another.

However, despite such moral and intellectual criticisms (especially by philosophers such as Plato), the Homeric picture of the gods as powerful *anthropomorphic* figures, for good and for ill, remained the basis for popular religion throughout antiquity. Herodotus may be exaggerating – Homer and Hesiod did not invent Greek religion, but rather adapted current religious beliefs to create their own worlds in which the gods play a part – yet his claim well captures the central role of poets in the development of Greek religion.

Let us begin by considering who the gods of the *Iliad* are. In contrast to the *Odyssey*, which has a smaller cast of divine characters (Zeus, Athena, and Poseidon), the *Iliad* features – in addition to Zeus, father of the gods – most of the major Olympians: Hera, Athena, Poseidon, Hermes, and Hephaestus (all supporting the Achaeans); Ares, Apollo, Artemis, and Aphrodite (supporting the Trojans). Although Dionysus and Demeter are mentioned (e.g. 6.132, 13.322), they do not feature in the action of the poem, and their absence may be explained by their status as particular benefactors of mankind (givers of wine and grain), which makes them less suitable as partisans of one side. The description of Zeus as 'the father of gods and men' (e.g. 1.544) highlights the particular emphasis in ancient Greek culture on the family structure of the gods (this idea is found in other Near Eastern religions, but is nowhere so prominent or developed as in the Greek pantheon). Moreover, the Greek gods display the same hierarchies and tensions that mark family dynamics among humans: thus, for example, Zeus indulges his favourite child, Athena (5.876-9), while Poseidon resents the power of his elder brother Zeus and is touchy about his own status (15.184-217). Zeus' authority over the divine family stems from his status as father, but it is ultimately bolstered by force: so instead of reasoning with the rebels Hera, Poseidon, and Athena, Zeus calls on the hundred-handed Briareos to intimidate them into submission (1.399-406), and he asserts his superiority by numerous threats of violence (e.g. 1.565-7, directed at Hera) and even by challenging all the gods to a massive tug of war (8.18-27).

To understand Greek religion, it is essential that we jettison inappropriate (especially Christian) conceptions of the divine as intrinsically kind and caring. For although the gods do care for humans, they are anything but selfless, and their honour (*timê*) is every bit as important to them as it is to the heroes. If a god's honour is damaged, as when Paris slights Hera and Athena by choosing Aphrodite as the most beautiful (24.25-30), they are no less relentless than the angriest of heroes in their pursuit of revenge, and their greater power means that their retribution is all the more terrifying. Thus Hera strikes a grim bargain with Zeus, offering up her three favourite cities for destruction (Argos, Sparta, and Mycenae) as long as Troy is obliterated (4.50-4), and she states her hatred of the Trojans in matter-of-fact terms (18.367): 'How could I not weave trouble for the Trojans, given my anger against them?'

As in real-life religion, the relationship between gods and humans in the *Iliad* is founded on mutual benefit: the gods delight in sacrifice and worship – so, for example, Apollo is pleased by the Achaeans' offerings, and by their singing and dancing in his honour, as he ends the plague (1.458-74) – and humans hope that in return their prayers will be heard. However, a deity is free to decline a prayer if it does not suit his or her larger purpose: the Trojans pray in vain for Athena's protection (6.305-11), and Zeus refuses to grant Achilles' prayer that Patroclus return safe from the fighting (16.249-52). Humans communicate with the gods through prayer, and the gods can respond via dreams, omens, prophecies, oracles, or direct intervention. The prominence of divine intervention in the *Iliad* is partly an indication of the gods' particular concern for their favourites: Aphrodite, for example, rescues Paris from the battlefield in a cloud of mist and deposits him in his bedroom (3.380-2), and Athena's care for Odysseus, so central to the *Odyssey*, is also a feature of the *Iliad* (10.245, 23.782-3). In the case of Paris, about to be killed by Menelaus, the goddess' interference highlights Paris' inferiority as a fighter, but divine involvement on the battlefield more often increases the hero's glory, as when Athena supports Achilles in his final duel with Hector (22.214-99).

Yet for all their exalted status (and at times divine parentage), the heroes are fundamentally different from the gods, and the most essential marker of the distance between them is death. Unlike the *Odyssey* and the poems of the Epic Cycle, the *Iliad* makes no mention of hero-cult (the posthumous worship of heroes as the powerful dead) or the possibility of immortality, and stresses thereby the absolute finality of death. The gulf between mortal and immortal is stark: the gods enjoy eternal vitality, humans face oblivion in Hades (there are no Isles of the Blessed or Elysium in the *Iliad*). This essential difference, the certainty of death for humans, is most powerfully expressed in a simile by Glaucus (6.146-9):

'As are the generations of leaves, so also are those of men:
the wind scatters the leaves on the ground, but the forest
burgeons and grows others when the season of spring comes round.
So with the generations of men, one grows and another ceases.'

However, it is paradoxically the very mortality of the heroes which gives them a seriousness and tragic intensity which the gods lack. For Sarpedon's speech to Glaucus on the nature of heroism (discussed in Chapter 3 above) argues that it is the prospect of death which gives the hero a reason to fight as he does (12.322-8):

'Friend, if we could escape from this war
and were sure to live forever, ageless and immortal,
I would not fight in the front ranks myself,
nor would I send you into battle where men win glory.
But now, since the spectres of death stand over us
in their thousands, which no mortal can flee from or escape,
let us go forward, and either give the glory to another man, or he to us.'

It follows that since the gods are 'sure to live forever, ageless and immortal', they face no risk of serious loss and so cannot be truly heroic. In other words, the power and immortality of the gods mean that they cannot display courage and endurance the way humans must, and so they are diminished in comparison to them. Moreover, because their actions lack tragic consequences (for themselves if not for humans), it is fitting that the gods 'who live at ease' (6.138 etc.) should themselves be the source of much humour in the poem, as when Sleep's qualms about deceiving Zeus are quickly overcome by Hera's promising him one of the Graces (14.270-6), or Athena mocks Aphrodite, who has been stabbed in the wrist by Diomedes, saying that she must have scratched her hand on a dress-pin (5.424-5). Indeed, Zeus himself laughs for joy at the sight of the gods fighting one another (21.389-90). As one ancient critic put it, 'Homer has done his best to make the men of the *Iliad* gods and the gods men' ([Longinus], *On the Sublime* 9.7).

From a divine perspective, the ephemerality of mortals makes it even less likely that any god would put himself or his interests at risk for their sake. Thus both Hephaestus, speaking to Hera (1.571-6), and Apollo, addressing Poseidon (21.460-7), argue that humans are not worth fighting over; Apollo, indeed, uses a similar simile of leaves and mortals to make his point. Naturally such an attitude can strike the human characters as aloof and uncaring, but the poem also makes clear the gods' concern for mortals despite their mortality: as Zeus says to Poseidon, 'I care for them, dying as they are' (20.21). Moreover, divine pity for human suffering is an essential part of the poem's resolution, as (most of) the gods intervene on behalf of Hector's helpless corpse, and Hermes tells Priam that 'Zeus, though far off, cares greatly and pities you' (24.174).

The gods pervade the poem to such an extent that they are sometimes presented as part of the human characters' decision to act in a particular way. Thus, for example, Diomedes says that Achilles will return to the fighting 'whenever the heart in his breast urges him to and a god incites him' (9.702-3). This pattern, often called 'double motivation', means that an action is capable of explanation on both a human and a divine level simultaneously. However, any given (human) character cannot know for sure if, or to what extent, another person is influenced by the gods, and so the idea of 'double motivation' is open to rhetorical manipulation: in other words, a character may try to exploit the idea of divine participation in order to escape the blame for a particular action or state of affairs. Thus, Paris cheekily tells Helen that Menelaus managed to defeat him in combat only because he had Athena's aid, when in fact (as we know) Athena did no such thing and it was Aphrodite who saved Paris (3.439-40). Or Agamemnon can attempt to save face by claiming that the goddess Atê (Delusion/Blindness) misled him and so he is not to blame for his disastrous quarrel with Achilles (19.85-136). However, it is important to emphasize that 'double motivation' never cancels out a human's responsibility for their actions or the state of affairs they have brought about. Thus, even in his brazen attempt to shift the blame, Agamemnon continues to admit responsibility for what he has done, and reaffirms his willingness to pay compensation to Achilles (19.137-44; cf. 9.116-20). What matters is the fact of human action, no matter how much a god was involved. So, for example, we are told of Patroclus' decision to press on towards Troy that 'it was Zeus who put the spirit to do so in his breast' (16.691), but it remains Patroclus' choice to ignore Achilles' instructions and he is responsible for his own death.

Just as any given action may be described in terms of human decision-making or divine involvement (or a combination of both), so it can also be presented as part of 'fate' (*moira, kêr, aisa*) or 'what is ordained' (*thesphaton, morsimon*). Homer is not a philosopher and does not get bogged down in technical debate about free will versus fate or predetermination. Instead he presents Zeus as having the ultimate control over what happens, so that in theory he could bring about an event 'contrary to what is fated', but only if he is willing to face the consequences. This is best illustrated by Zeus' relationship to the ultimate 'fate' of all men, namely death. For Zeus twice considers sparing a mortal from his fated end, Sarpedon in Book 16 and Hector in Book 22. But in each case he is warned not to do so, since (as Hera argues in the first scene, endorsed by Athena in the second) human mortality is a basic part of the cosmic order, and if Zeus upsets this he risks anarchy, as all the gods would seek to make their children or favourites immortal (16.439-49, 22.177-81). Zeus is not the same thing as Fate, but he is the god with the power to reveal it, as his major prophecies make clear, encompassing the deaths of Sarpedon and Patroclus, Achilles' return to the fighting, the death of Hector, and the fall of Troy (8.469-77, 15.64-77). Homer creates a striking visual symbol of Zeus' peculiarly close relationship to 'what is ordained' when the fates (*kêres*) of Achilles and Hector are weighed in 'the scales of Zeus' and Hector's sinks down (22.208-13).

Zeus' unique knowledge of 'fate' is part of his wider plan for both gods and mortals. This plan is encapsulated in the *Dios boulê*, or 'plan of Zeus', which is expressed in the opening lines of the *Iliad*, as the poet summarizes the impact of Achilles' anger by saying *Dios d'eteleieto boulê*, 'and the plan of Zeus was fulfilled' (1.5). The phrase sets Achilles' anger in its larger cosmic context, since the *Dios boulê* is not limited to one hero's anger or even the story of the Trojan War, but embraces all actions and events (human and divine). In other words, the plot of the *Iliad* is merely one embodiment of Zeus' overarching will. The expression 'plan of Zeus' is intentionally (and usefully) vague, since it sums up Zeus' ultimate, but not entirely knowable, power over both gods and mortals, and emphasizes that Zeus' plan is only gradually revealed to them (and to us) as the poem unfolds. In other words, Zeus' will is always in process, an idea underlined by the proem's imperfect tense *eteleieto*, which strictly means 'was in the process of being fulfilled'. In a narrow sense the primary (local) referent of the *Dios boulê* in the *Iliad* proem is Zeus' plan to bring honour to Achilles by helping the Trojans (e.g. 1.508-9, 11.79, 16.121, 17.331-2). But at the same time Zeus has a larger plan for the destruction of Troy, and must therefore balance his initial promise to Thetis against his desire to preserve the Achaeans: 'he [Zeus] did not want the Achaean army to perish utterly in front of Troy, but was bringing glory to Thetis and her strong-hearted son' (13.348-50). Moreover, Zeus' promise to Thetis is merely one instance of a much larger phenomenon, namely Zeus' need to take into account the wider divine society, where all the gods have their own favourites and their own plans. It is a mark of Zeus' success in this respect that the order which results from the competing wills of the gods is ultimately identified with the larger 'plan of Zeus', which shapes the narrative of the entire poem.

Zeus (together with the other gods) not only maintains order on a cosmic level, but also enforces justice among humans. While the gods' role in the achievement of justice is very clear in the *Odyssey* (where Odysseus punishes the suitors with the help of Athena and the approval of Zeus), its role in the *Iliad* has not always been appreciated, and many scholars have even argued that the Iliadic gods are not concerned with justice. However, the gods' undoubted selfishness and occasional frivolity (which so appalled philosophers such as Xenophanes, Heraclitus, and Plato) does not mean that they cannot also act as enforcers of positive and disinterested moral values such as justice. Thus, for example, Zeus is said to punish a city whose rulers disregard justice (16.386-8):

He grows angry with men and is furious with them,
because by violence they give crooked judgements in their assembly,
and drive out justice, with no concern for punishment from the gods.

Far from being amoral powers, the Iliadic gods enforce a basic ethical
system, whose ultimate guarantor is Zeus, and this moral pattern is most
clearly seen in the gods' relationship to the fall of Troy.

Multiple human decisions contribute to the fall of Troy, ranging from
the initial Judgement of Paris (24.25-30) through to Hector's failure to
preserve his people (22.99-110), but all involve the gods in some way. If
divine anger against Troy rested solely on Hera and Athena's defeat in
the Judgement of Paris, we might think the gods rather petty. However,
whatever the sensitivities of individual gods (who, we must remember,
have as much right to avenge their damaged honour as mortals do), the
poem makes it abundantly clear that Trojan suffering stems primarily
from Trojan mistakes rather than divine vindictiveness. In the opening
scene of the *Odyssey* the same principle is said by Zeus to apply to all
human suffering (1.32-43). In other words, the fall of Troy, which is Zeus'
will too, is shown to embody a basic concept of justice (and one shared
by both Homeric epics).

It is a Trojan, Paris, who begins the war, and his voyage to Sparta is
described as 'the beginning of misery for all the Trojans and for himself'
(5.63-4). Just after the duel between Paris and Menelaus, as Helen and
Paris go to bed with each other, Paris recalls their first sexual encounter
(3.441-6):

'But come – let us go to bed and find delight in love;
for never before has desire so enveloped my mind,
not even when I first stole you away from lovely Lacedaemon
and sailed off with you in my seafaring ships,
and on the island of Cranaë took you to bed and made love to you –
that was nothing to how I desire you now and sweet longing seizes
    me.'

The original offence, the abduction of Helen, is thus re-enacted within the
narrative of the *Iliad* itself. Menelaus links this crime to the eventual
destruction of the Trojans (13.622-7):

'You Trojans cannot get enough of insulting and disgracing others –
as you insulted me, you shameless dogs, with no fear
in your hearts for the harsh anger of loud-thundering Zeus,

god of host and guest, who will one day destroy your lofty city.
For you made off with my wedded wife and many possessions besides,
for no reason at all, since you had been given a friendly welcome by her.'

The added detail that Paris stole Menelaus' property as well as his wife underlines the Trojan's outrageous violation of the protocols of hospitality. Nor is it only the Greeks who disapprove of Paris' actions: Hector describes them as worthy of stoning (3.56-7) and wishes he would die at once (6.281-2), while the Trojans, so the narrator tells us, all hated Paris 'like black death' (3.454).

The principle of justified Trojan punishment is seen every bit as clearly in the account of the broken truce in Book 4 and Priam's disastrous reaction to it in Book 7. As the head of his community, Priam makes the truce on the Trojans' behalf (3.105-10, 250-2). Then, following a solemn sacrifice, both the Achaeans and the Trojans call upon Zeus to punish the side that breaks the oaths ratifying the truce (3.298-301). Nonetheless, the Trojan Pandarus attempts to kill Menelaus, and his crime serves as a recapitulation of Trojan guilt. Although Athena and Hera promote the breaking of the truce, with Zeus' consent (4.64-72), the principle of 'double motivation' means that Pandarus' culpability is not diminished. Athena tempts Pandarus with the thought of the gifts he might win from Paris if he kills Menelaus (4.93-103), but she does not compel him to act as he does. Indeed, Pandarus is described as 'thoughtless' (4.104) and so just the kind of man likely to commit such a foolish act. Moreover, the blame for Pandarus' crime extends to the Trojans in general, since Pandarus' comrades support him in his attempt to kill Menelaus (4.113-15):

His noble companions held their shields in front of him,
so that the warrior sons of the Achaeans could not rush him
before he had hit Menelaus, Atreus' warrior son.

The Trojans thus share collective responsibility for the breaking of the truce and the violation of their oaths.

The Trojans' responsibility for the broken truce is compounded by Priam's personal failure to return Helen after the duel. The advice given by 'wise Antenor' not only constitutes an admission of Trojan guilt but also highlights Priam's imminent misjudgement (7.350-3):

'Come now, let us give Argive Helen and her possessions with her
back to the sons of Atreus, for them to take away. We are fighting now

after cheating over our sworn oaths; so I do not think
that any good will come to us, unless we do as I say.'

However, when Paris declares himself willing to return only the goods
taken from Sparta, 'I will not give the woman back' (7.362), Priam's
complicity is clear. The Trojan herald Idaeus, charged by Priam with
relaying the response of the Trojan assembly, underlines the king's great
error in turning a blind eye to his son's crime (7.389-93):

'The possessions that Alexander brought in his hollow ships
to Troy – if only he had died before he did! –
all these he is willing to give back, and to add more from his own stores.
But the wedded wife of glorious Menelaus
he says he will not give back, though the Trojans certainly urge him to.'

It could not be clearer that Priam has made a disastrous mistake, allowing
Paris to defy the oath, and doing so in the face of popular disapproval. No
less than Paris, Priam is responsible for the destruction of Troy, his city.
He acts wrongly, and he – and everyone else who depends on him – must
suffer the consequences.

As the poem progresses there are several more indications of Trojan
wrongdoing. During Agamemnon's *aristeia* in Book 11 he comes upon
two sons of Antimachus, a Trojan 'who in return for gold from Alexander,
a splendid gift, was most opposed to giving Helen back to fair-haired
Menelaus' (11.123-5). The revelation that Paris has bribed a fellow Trojan
brings disgrace on their whole community, but Antimachus' own conduct
emerges as particularly blameworthy, for as Agamemnon says
(11.138-42):

'If you are truly the sons of war-minded Antimachus,
who once in the Trojan assembly urged that Menelaus,
who had come on an embassy with godlike Odysseus,
should be killed on the spot and not be allowed back to the Achaeans,
then now you will pay for your father's abominable outrage.'

Antimachus' attempt to have an ambassador killed, though unsuccessful,
reinforces the sense of Trojan treachery calling forth punishment.
Moreover, this pattern is shown to extend back beyond the current
generation. Poseidon, puzzled by Apollo's continuing support for the
Trojans, reminds him of how Laomedon had cheated them both of proper
payment after they built a wall around Troy and tended the king's cattle

(21.441-57). When Poseidon sent a sea-monster to punish the Trojans, Heracles destroyed it, but he in turn was defrauded of his reward by Laomedon and took his revenge by sacking Troy (5.648-51, 20.144-8). Nevertheless, Poseidon's anger against Troy remains unappeased, and so the Trojans, the descendants of Laomedon, can be seen to be paying for his crimes as well as their own.

The fall of Troy is thus a manifestation of justice, albeit a harsh kind of justice, on both the divine and human level. Multiple Trojan mistakes contribute to the destruction of their community, but none more so than Paris' initial offence and Priam's subsequent failure to undo it. We see Priam's inability to face his own responsibilities as leader when he says to Helen, 'You are not to blame in my eyes, it is the gods who are to blame, who roused tear-laden war for me with the Achaeans' (3.164-5). Priam is trying here to comfort Helen by blaming the gods for what has happened (in another rhetorical manipulation of 'double motivation'), but Helen rejects his face-saving words and emphasizes her own share of the blame, insisting that she should have died rather than abandon her family, and reviling herself as 'bitch-faced' (3.171-80). Helen's vehement acceptance of her own guilt underlines not only how tendentious Priam's claim is, but also (because he is too exculpatory) how much of the blame he must share himself.

We should beware of not allowing our genuine pity for the Trojans to obscure the fact of their wrongdoing. For it would be easy to focus on the men's fighting in defence of their wives and children, or on the killing and degradation of the latter as war-captives, and be tempted thereby to see only 'the pity of war'. But while the brutality of war is an undeniable and essential aspect of the *Iliad*, the poem also presents the Trojans as both pitiable *and* culpable. In other words, it is possible for an audience to feel compassion even for merited suffering, and the *Iliad* guides its audience to see not only the Trojans' faults, but also the gods' role in punishing them. The Trojan people pay the ultimate price for the flaws of their leaders, but this is still (in Greek terms) a manifestation of divine and human *dikê* ('justice'), because crimes such as Paris' cannot go unpunished, while failures of leadership such as Priam's are bound to damage the community.

Divine justice is eventually served on the Trojans, in accordance with the 'plan of Zeus'. Although Hera complains that Zeus 'takes the Trojans' side in the fighting' (1.521), this is a sign of her impatience for the destruction of her enemies rather than Zeus' actual viewpoint. As Zeus makes clear, Troy is 'fated' to fall, but Hera and Athena cannot control that process (e.g. 8.5-40); their personal hatred of Troy has to operate within a larger moral framework in which punishment is justified because of human crimes. As with the human audience, Zeus' feelings of pity at Troy's destruction and his conviction that the fall of Troy is right are not mutually exclusive. Zeus speaks on one occasion as if he wants to save Troy, but his real motive is evidently to provoke Hera and Athena and so bring about the breaking of the truce (4.5-19). He also makes clear his strong affection for the Trojans, because they offer him lavish sacrifices (4.44-9), but this does not change the fact that he approves of Troy's fall, since Zeus can love Troy and still think it right that the Trojans be punished. Zeus does not express any happiness at Troy's fall, but his approval is not only implicit in the narrative itself but also integral to the larger moral order of which he is the ultimate enforcer. Zeus' desire that Troy should fall (15.69-71) is predicated upon his belief that it is right.

In conclusion, the lives of gods and mortals are intertwined throughout the *Iliad*, not least because the gods are essential to the poem's exploration of human heroism and suffering. The 'plan of Zeus' is realized through the actions and reactions of others, including other gods. Thus, as Achilles prepares to re-enter the fighting, Zeus assembles the gods and encourages them to help the side of their choice, so that Achilles may not sack Troy 'beyond what is fated' (20.23-30); but it is clear that the pro-Trojan gods will eventually have to give way, since Troy must fall. Thus the city's demise is presented as part of an impartial system of divinely supported justice in which both Trojans and Achaeans face the consequences of their misdeeds.

Chapter 5

War and Family Life

This chapter will analyse the *Iliad*'s presentation of gender roles, showing how these roles (like all relationships in human society) are tested and distorted by violence, and will also explore the depiction of war in the poem. Hector's reassuring words to Andromache, 'war will be the concern of men' (6.492), will emerge as naïve, since the poem makes clear that the consequences of men's defeat in battle wreak their greatest havoc on the lives of women. As well as illustrating the interdependence of men and women (in their duties, rights, and responsibilities), this chapter will consider how the *Iliad* offers positive and negative paradigms of male and female behaviour, principally in the contrast between Hector's relationship with Andromache and Paris' with Helen. Finally, although much scholarly literature continues to focus on women as problematic figures within the epic's martial context, we shall see that the *Iliad*, like the *Odyssey*, endorses women's authority (as much as men's) and affirms their value to society.

The *Iliad*'s focus on warfare, heroism, and comradeship is self-evident, but it would be a mistake to think that masculinity or the bonds between men were the be all and end all of the poem. And yet, while the 'domestic' side of the *Odyssey* has long been appreciated, the *Iliad*'s presentation of women and the social divisions between male and female has been relatively neglected, and often reduced to a simple polarization of male = public space/war *versus* female = domestic space/peace. So before we look at the different gender roles and how they relate to one another, let us begin by considering what the poem has to say about men and women in their own right, beginning with its depiction of manliness.

The masculine ideal is a blend of strength and intelligence. The poem, like much Greek art, foregrounds the strength and beauty of the male body. Thus, for example, when Helen identifies for Priam the leading Achaean warriors in Book 3, the heroes' individual physical traits are highlighted: Agamemnon is 'handsome and dignified' and 'has the look of a king' (3.169-70), Odysseus is shorter than Agamemnon 'but broader in his shoulders and chest to look upon' (3.194), Menelaus is 'tall and broad-shouldered' (3.210), while Ajax, the 'bulwark of the Achaeans', is simply 'huge' (3.229). Achilles boasts of his own outstanding physique and beauty as he intimidates the terrified Lycaon (21.108): 'Do you not see what kind of a man I am, how handsome and mighty?' However, just as it is an affliction to lack beauty – the sheer physical repulsiveness of Thersites, the poem's only ugly character, is emphatic: he is bandy-legged, lame, with hunched shoulders, a pointy head and only a few wisps of hair (2.216-19) – so it is a source of blame to be merely beautiful (but lack strength) or too concerned with one's looks: thus Nireus is described in the Catalogue of Achaean forces as 'the handsomest man that came to Ilium of all the Danaans, except for the incomparable son of Peleus, but he was a weakling, and few people followed him' (2.673-5), while Hector attacks Paris as a 'supremely beautiful, woman-crazy seducer' whose 'hair and beauty' are no replacement for 'strength and courage' (3.39-57). The ideal man unites strength and intelligence, so that he can excel in the two major arenas of heroic excellence, the battlefield and the assembly, and become, as Phoenix reminds Achilles (9.443), 'both a speaker of words and a doer of deeds' (see Chapter 3 above). Different heroes possess these qualities to different degrees – thus Odysseus acknowledges Achilles' peerless strength, but asserts his superior judgement, 'since I am older than you and know more' (19.216-19) – but the ideal man will excel both physically and mentally.

Like men, Iliadic women are admired for their beauty and skills, albeit skills exercised within the limitations of women's lives, which are largely connected to the house of their father or husband. When Hector does not find Andromache at home, he assumes she has gone 'to the house of one of my sisters or my brothers' finely-robed wives, or to Athena's temple, where the other lovely-haired women of Troy are seeking to appease the fearsome goddess' (6.378-80). The importance of female beauty is embodied within the formulaic language of the poem, where women are typically 'finely-robed', 'lovely-haired', 'deep-girdled', 'fair-cheeked', and so on. But even more so than with male attractiveness, female beauty is double-edged and can be disastrous (as Helen's experience shows), not least because it makes a woman prey to sexual subjection if her freedom is lost. So Agamemnon, harshly rejecting the supplication of Chryses, speaks of the old man's daughter 'going back and forth at the loom and serving my bed' (1.31). Nonetheless, as with men, female beauty is ideally combined with brains and skills, as when Agamemnon (no less crassly) says he prefers the captive Chryseis to his own wife Clytemnestra, 'since she is in no way inferior to her in figure or in beauty, nor in mind or handicrafts' (1.114-15).

Mention of Chryseis reminds us that in comparing the gender roles of men and women, it is important we compare like with like, e.g. husbands with wives, rather than free men with female war-captives. This is not to deny that the role of female captives as symbols of male honour reveals a significant aspect of women's experience; however, such captives are not of the same status as wives, and so to focus on them risks confusing issues of status with those of gender. So, for example, while the poem's initial male contention over Chryseis and Briseis may echo the original dispute over Helen, only the latter can tell us about the relationships of men and women in their normative role as wives and husbands. (This distinction can, however, be blurred by the characters themselves, for rhetorical reasons, as when Achilles describes Briseis as 'my wife, my heart's love' (9.336) in order to emphasize the damage to *his* honour which her removal represents.) Therefore, since our focus is on gender dynamics rather than status (or loss of status), we shall look at married couples like Hector and Andromache rather than enforced unions like Agamemnon and Chryseis or Achilles and Briseis.

The most famous and revealing passage for the definition of gender roles comes in Hector's meeting with Andromache in Book 6. The scene is prepared for when Sarpedon speaks to Hector of the wife and infant son he has left behind in Lycia (5.480, 688), so that we think of Hector's own family as he returns to Troy to urge the women of the city to appease Athena. In his meetings with Hecuba, Paris, Helen, and Andromache we see Hector as son, brother, and (most fully and intensely) as husband and father. Each meeting emphasizes his commitment to his family and his people, but also stresses that he must risk his life to protect theirs. Hector dismisses his wife's appeal for him to remain safely in Troy, and as he returns to the battlefield, he sends Andromache back home, with words that reaffirm the difference between the genders (6.490-3):

'Go back to the house and see to your own tasks,
the loom and the distaff, and tell your maids
to set about their work as well. War will be the concern of men,
of all those who were born in Ilium, and mine above all.'

On the one hand, Hector's words endorse an ideal of female behaviour, focused on the proper running of the household. On the other, they also respond to Andromache's offer of military advice (6.433-9) by reminding her that war is not the concern of women, and she should return to the proper sphere of female activity and skill. In one sense there is nothing unusual or controversial about Hector's advice, since the *Iliad*, like Greek culture generally, does operate in terms of separate areas of male (public/military) and female (private/domestic) activity. However, the wider context encourages us to see Hector's rigid division between the two spheres as too simplistic, since, as we shall see, they are interconnected in many ways.

This passage is often read as a rebuke, but we are in fact told that Hector's intention is to comfort Andromache (484-9). So in saying that war will be men's concern, Hector is trying to reassure his wife of his protective power. But his own speech has already made clear the extent of female suffering, as he details the traumas and indignities that Andromache and the other women of Troy will endure when Troy falls (456-8):

> 'You will live in Argos, weaving at the loom at another woman's command,
> and carrying water from the spring Messeïs or Hypereia,
> much against your will; and a harsh compulsion will lie upon you.'

Though Hector cannot bring himself to express it directly, this 'harsh compulsion' will also involve Andromache's sexual subjugation by another man. (Women suffer the consequences of war in a particularly degrading way, as when Nestor urges the Achaeans not to return home until each of them has raped a Trojan woman to avenge 'the struggles and groans of Helen' (2.354-6).) In other words, Hector himself has already drawn attention to the ways in which war destroys the lives of women, and this makes his claim that 'war will be the concern of men' seem hopelessly naïve – he is, to his credit, trying to comfort his wife, but his words are wishful thinking nonetheless. This is underlined by the scene in which the news of Hector's death reaches Andromache: she is weaving (as he instructed her to) and preparing a bath for his return from the battle (22.440-6), but the domestic scene is shattered by the loss of her husband. For all Hector's good intentions, the world of war cannot be separated from that of women. Moreover, the defensive spirit of Andromache's tactical advice is proven correct, and Hector later regrets his decision not to stay within the walls of Troy (22.99-110).

The meeting between Andromache and Hector also brings out the dependence of women on men that is a basic feature of ancient Greek society. Achilles had killed Andromache's father and seven brothers, and enslaved her mother, so that Hector is all she has (6.429-30):

> 'Hector, you are my father and honoured mother
> and brother, and you are my strong husband.'

But for all its tragic intensity, Andromache's reliance on Hector mirrors the dependence of all ancient women on the men around them. Their world is dominated by men, upon whose protection they rely. Even Helen, one of the most powerful of mortal women because of her awesome beauty, has no say in the Trojan assembly in Book 7 that debates whether to return her to her husband – like any other woman, her fate is determined by men. This pattern is also reflected on the divine level, for although goddesses enjoy a degree of power and independence denied to mortal women, they too live within a society and family shaped by patriarchal authority. Thus, Hera is annoyed by Zeus' extra-marital affairs, but is powerless to stop him (14.313-28), while Calypso complains of the double standard that allows gods to have mortal lovers, but criticizes goddesses when they do the same (*Odyssey* 5.118-29). Zeus is a man, and his will prevails.

However, despite these fundamental cultural limitations on female activity and authority, the *Iliad* also insists on the positive value of women's roles. It is easy to bemoan ancient women's constrained existence, but such an approach does not help us understand the *Iliad* (or any other ancient text), and risks obscuring the important point that women's excellence is presented in the *Iliad* as complementary to men's and no less essential to a flourishing human society. A harmonious marriage is seen as central to a good life. On the shield of Achilles are depicted two cities, one at peace, the other at war, and the first characteristic feature of the city at peace is its celebration of marriage (18.490-6). The cultural ideal of harmony between the sexes is summed up in the notion of *homophrosynê*, or 'like-mindedness', which Odysseus hopes the Phaeacian princess Nausicaa will enjoy (*Odyssey* 6.180-5):

'May the gods give you all that your heart desires,
a husband and home, and may they bestow harmony (*homophrosynê*),
which is a noble thing. For nothing is stronger or better than this,
when a man and woman make their home together
in harmony of mind (*homophroneonte noêmasin*): this is a great grief
        to their enemies,
a joy to their friends, and a source of high repute for themselves.'

This 'harmony of mind' is best illustrated in the *Iliad* by the contrasting marriages of Hector and Andromache on the one hand, and Paris and Helen or Menelaus and Helen on the other.

As we have seen, Andromache fails in her attempt to persuade Hector to stay in Troy, but this difference in attitude does not entail that their relationship lacks 'harmony'. For *homophrosynê* does not mean that men and women must think or behave in the same way; on the contrary, it consists of men and women working in their own sphere and respecting the other party's legitimate claim to authority in their typical roles, so that their activities and responsibilities interlink and support one another. So in trying to get Hector to stay in Troy, Andromache is exercising her rights as a wife and defending the claims of the household. For she is right when she says to Hector 'your own heroic spirit (*menos*) will destroy you' (6.407), and she knows that his death will destroy her and their son's life as well. Thus, it is Andromache's duty to remind Hector of his responsibilities towards his family, as his opening words to her acknowledge, 'Wife, I too feel concern for these things' (6.441), even if her doing so accentuates the difficulty of Hector's predicament, since he must decide between his conflicting obligations to his family and his own heroic values (6.441-3):

> 'Wife, I too feel concern for these things. But I would feel terrible
> shame before the Trojans and the Trojan women with their trailing
>   robes
> if like a coward I were to skulk away from the fighting.'

In short, Hector and Andromache do what comes 'naturally' to them: she insists on the well-being of their family and tries to delay her husband from battle, he looks more to the public pressures of male heroism. Tragically, however, although they complement one another perfectly as husband and wife, their relationship is threatened by war, which destroys the conventions of normal life.

By contrast, the relationships Helen has with Paris and Menelaus are profoundly lacking in 'harmony'. Whereas Hector and Andromache act in archetypally male and female ways, the gender roles are reversed in the preceding scene with Paris and Helen, where instead of restraining Paris (as a wife normally would), Helen must shame him into fighting (6.349-51):

> 'But since the gods have ordained these evils,
> I wish that I was the wife of a better man,
> one who understood what disgrace is and the many shaming things that
>   people say.'

Whereas a proper man (like Hector) is aware of his duty to the wider community, Paris is not, and has to be reminded of it by a woman. His deficiency as both a man and a warrior are clear. Thus the failings of Helen and Paris' relationship affirm by contrast both the heroism of Hector and the 'harmony' that exists between him and Andromache. Finally, Helen's other relationship is no more exemplary: while Menelaus sees himself as fighting 'to avenge Helen's struggles and groans' (2.590), we get a far more ambiguous picture of Helen's attitude to Paris, especially when, despite her protestations and self-loathing, she goes to bed with him in a scene that recalls their initial encounter (3.441-6, quoted in Chapter 3 above).

The fact that we can compare and contrast these Trojan and Achaean relationships reminds us that the two peoples are presented as fundamentally alike. With the possible exception of Priam's 'polygamy' (8.302-5, 21.84-5, 24.495-7; he has 50 sons by various *gynaikes*, but the word can mean both 'wives' and 'mistresses', so it is not clear if multiple *marriages* are meant), which is in any case hardly prominent, both sides observe the same basic social customs (oath-swearing, supplication, guest-friendship, and so on) and worship the same gods. Similarly, although there are a few references to the fact that the Trojans' allies must in reality have spoken a multiplicity of languages (2.804, 867, 4.437-8), the allies and the Trojans themselves are depicted as speaking Greek, which again stresses the lack of ethnic differentiation. So instead of demonizing the Trojans as inferior 'barbarians', Homer has chosen to underline their similarity to the Achaeans. (We now say 'Greeks', but Homer refers to the whole army using the collective names Achaeans, Danaans, or Argives, each name referring to a Panhellenic force united by its mission to punish Trojan crimes.) The effect of this ethnic assimilation is two-fold: on the one hand, it makes the Trojans seem all the more sympathetic (to a Greek audience); on the other hand, the Trojans' similarity to the Achaeans underlines how far they have fallen short of shared standards of behaviour in not opposing Paris' retention of Helen (for other examples of Trojan treachery, see Chapter 4 above).

Moreover, the poem as a whole makes clear the fundamental superiority of the Achaeans in battle, and thus affirms Achaean 'manliness'. Far more Trojans are killed in the course of the poem, despite the fact that on the second and third days of battle (Books 8 and 11-18) the Trojans are in the ascendancy, pushing the Achaeans back into their camp, breaching their defensive wall, and setting fire to their ships. Overall there are 189 named Trojans and Trojan allies killed, as against only 54 Achaeans. Moreover, the Trojans are four times more likely than the Achaeans to panic and flee (rather than stage a calm retreat), and only Trojans are taken prisoner or need to be rescued by gods. The Achaeans' superior discipline is heralded when the two armies are first described assembling for battle at the start of Book 3: the Trojans are compared to screeching cranes, 'but the Achaeans advanced in silence, breathing valour, their hearts intent on defending one another' (3.8-9). Whereas the similes in the battle narratives tend to compare the Trojans to flocks of sheep and herds of cattle, the Achaeans are likened to fierce fighting animals such as lions and boars. As soon as the gods leave the battlefield at the beginning of Book 6, the Achaeans show their military superiority, breaking the Trojan ranks and driving them back towards the city. By contrast, the Trojans enjoy major success only when Achilles is withdrawn from the fighting and Zeus helps them gain the upper hand, and when the other major Achaean warriors are wounded. Finally, when the gods clash in Books 20 and 21, it is the pro-Achaean gods who have the best of the fighting. This pro-Achaean 'bias' should not surprise us, since it is natural for Homer's Greek audience to enjoy Greek success (and this aspect of the poem enhances its appeal to a Panhellenic audience). This does not make the poem anti-Trojan or annul our sympathy for the Trojans, since they are still presented as brave and committed fighters, but it is clear the Achaeans are in that respect superior.

The Achaeans' martial pre-eminence reminds us that to fully understand the *Iliad* we must balance the suffering caused by war against the glory that comes from success in it. The cost of war is most powerfully encapsulated in its effects on Hector and his family, whose experience is used to represent the relationship of all warriors to their loved ones and dependents. Andromache and Astyanax are symbolic of war widows and orphans everywhere, and Troy's impending destruction stands as the prototype of war's effects on civilized community life. The epithets used most frequently of war ('tear-filled', 'man-slaying', 'painful', 'hateful', 'evil') underline the grief it causes, an attitude summed up by the poet when he says of one violent clash (between the Cretan leader Idomeneus and the Trojans), 'it would be a hard-hearted man indeed who could take pleasure in seeing such toil and not feel grief' (13.343-4). The obituaries of dead warriors highlight pathetic details such as bereaved parents and the loss of youthful beauty and vitality, and the poem ends with an intense expression of pity, as Achilles identifies with the sufferings of his enemy. Nonetheless, for all its emphasis on the negative effects of war, the poem also reflects the Greeks' admiration for those who are good at it. War is not only an evil which destroys families and annihilates cities, but also the supreme test of heroic excellence and the source of 'deathless glory' (*kleos aphthiton*, 9.413). As modern readers, it is tempting to overplay the poem's critique of war and see it as a proto-pacifist work, but nothing could be more anachronistic or misleading. For the poem delights in and celebrates battlefield prowess even as it foregrounds the miseries and losses of war. Homer presents the complexity of war, not a one-dimensional and lazy critique of it. War's complex nature is perhaps best embodied in the shield of Achilles in Book 18, with its two cities (one at war, the other at peace), a wondrous and divinely wrought object which reminds us that war is only one aspect of life, that no sane person would prefer war to peace, but also that war is sometimes necessary. The *Iliad*'s balanced presentation of war as a basic part of life, a source of honour, and a great evil, is neither paradoxical nor a relic of 'archaic' thought, but an attitude that we too can relate to, as we hope that our society will avoid armed conflict, but still venerate our war dead.

In conclusion, the *Iliad* shows the interdependence of men and women in their rights and responsibilities. It also endorses women's authority (as much as men's) and affirms their value to society. This is powerfully illustrated in a simile used to describe the wounded Agamemnon, where his sharp pains are compared to those of a woman in childbirth (11.269-72). While scholars usually see this comparison as undermining Agamemnon, it is rather, I would argue, a measure of the seriousness with which women's contribution to society was regarded. It is a tribute to the physical endurance of women and an instance of the 'childbirth is to women as war is to men' equivalence that we see most famously deployed by Euripides' Medea: 'I would rather stand three times with a shield in battle than give birth once' (*Medea* 250-1). Positive and negative paradigms of marriage (Hector and Andromache, Paris/Menelaus and Helen) illustrate the benefits of *homophrosynê*, a harmonious partnership between the sexes. Like the *Odyssey*, the *Iliad* shows the legitimacy of women's concerns and their spheres of authority. Andromache fails to persuade Hector to stay in Troy, but her appeal is presented as valid and in line with the responsibilities of a wife and mother. Ideally men and women will respect gender boundaries and meet their obligations, which are mutually supportive: Paris and Helen show what happens when they fail to do so. The *Iliad* also shows how gender roles (like all human relationships) are distorted by war, so that Hector's adage 'war will be the concern of men' emerges as poignantly naïve, since the consequences of defeat in the male arena of war wreak their greatest destruction on women and their families. Finally, by setting the Trojan war within the wider context of human norms, including those of family life, which the war itself disrupts, the *Iliad* underlines the benefits of peace and the values of civilized life.

Epilogue

In the *Homeric Hymn to Apollo*, written long after Homer in the early sixth century BC, the bard urges the girls of Delos to reply, should anyone ask them who their favourite poet is, 'It is a blind man, and he lives on rocky Chios, and all of his songs remain forever the best' (172-3). Leaving aside the questionable biographical details (see Chapter 1 above), we can still agree with the hymn's estimation of Homer's success in creating the *Iliad*, the greatest poem of Western culture.

Suggestions for Further Reading

Given the vast amount of scholarship on the *Iliad*, this section must be highly selective. It is limited to works in English, with the aim of expanding on the core topics covered in the book.

Texts, commentaries, and translations

The most widely used text is the Oxford Classical Text, edited by D.B. Monro and T.W. Allen (Oxford University Press). The best and most detailed modern edition is that by M.L. West, *Homeri Ilias*, 2 vols (Teubner: K.G. Saur Verlag, 1998-2000). The fullest commentary is that edited in six volumes by G.S. Kirk, J.B. Hainsworth, R. Janko, M.W. Edwards, and N. Richardson (Cambridge University Press, 1985-93). Excellent translations are available in the Penguin Classics series by Martin Hammond (1987) and the Oxford World's Classics by Anthony Verity (2011).

General works

D.L. Cairns (ed.), *Oxford Readings in Homer's Iliad* (Oxford University Press, 2001) brings together a collection of classic articles, with a detailed and wide-ranging Introduction surveying modern Homeric scholarship. Essays on all aspects of the poem may be found in two major Companions: I. Morris and B. Powell (eds), *A New Companion to Homer* (Brill, 1997) and R. Fowler (ed.), *The Cambridge Companion to Homer* (Cambridge University Press, 2004). Entries on a myriad topics are contained in M. Finkelberg (ed.), *The Homer Encyclopedia*, 3 vols (Wiley-Blackwell, 2011). R.B. Rutherford, *Homer* (New Surveys in the Classics No. 26: Oxford University Press, 1996) offers an expert overview of key issues (in both *Iliad* and *Odyssey*). There are many general Introductions to the *Iliad*; three of the most readable and rewarding are M.W. Edwards, *Homer: Poet of the Iliad* (Johns Hopkins University Press, 1987), M. Mueller, *The Iliad*, 2nd edn (Bristol Classical Press, 2009), and O. Taplin, *Homeric Soundings: The Shaping of the Iliad* (Oxford University Press, 1992).

Chapter 1. Homer and Early Greek Epic

J. Burgess, *The Tradition of the Trojan War in Homer and the Epic Cycle* (Johns Hopkins University Press, 2001)

A. Ford, *Homer: The Poetry of the Past* (Cornell University Press, 1992)

R. Fowler, 'The Homeric Question', in R. Fowler (ed.), *The Cambridge Companion to Homer* (Cambridge University Press, 2004) 220-32

T. Gantz, *Early Greek Myth: A Guide to Literary and Artistic Sources* (Johns Hopkins University Press, 1993)

B. Graziosi, *Inventing Homer: The Early Reception of Epic* (Cambridge University Press, 2002)

B. Graziosi and J. Haubold, *Homer: The Resonance of Epic* (Duckworth, 2005)

A. Kelly, *A Referential Commentary and Lexicon to Homer, Iliad VIII* (Oxford University Press, 2007)

J. Latacz, *Troy and Homer: Towards a Solution of an Old Mystery*, tr. K. Windle and R. Ireland (Oxford University Press, 2004)

A. Snodgrass, *Homer and the Artists: Text and Picture in Early Greek Art* (Cambridge University Press, 1998)

W.G. Thalmann, *Conventions of Form and Thought in Early Greek Epic Poetry* (Johns Hopkins University Press, 1984)

M.L. West, *The East Face of Helicon: West Asiatic Elements in Greek Poetry and Myth* (Oxford University Press, 1997)

M.L. West, *The Making of the Iliad: Disquisition and Analytical Commentary* (Oxford University Press, 2010)

Chapter 2. Language, Style, and Structure

E.J. Bakker, *Pointing at the Past: From Formula to Performance in Homeric Poetics* (Center for Hellenic Studies, 2005)

B. Fenik, *Typical Battle Scenes in the Iliad: Studies in the Narrative Techniques of Homeric Battle Description* (Steiner Verlag, 1968)

J.M. Foley, *Homer's Traditional Art* (Penn State University Press, 1999)

J. Griffin, 'Words and Speakers in Homer', *Journal of Hellenic Studies* 106 (1986) 36-57

J.B. Hainsworth, *The Flexibility of the Homeric Formula* (Oxford University Press, 1968)

B. Heiden, *Homer's Cosmic Fabrication: Choice and Design in the Iliad* (Oxford University Press, 2008)

G. Horrocks, 'Homer's Dialect', in I. Morris and B. Powell (eds), *A New Companion to Homer* (Brill, 1997) 193-217

R. Janko, *Homer, Hesiod and the Hymns: Diachronic Development in Epic Diction* (Cambridge University Press, 1982)

B. Louden, *The Iliad: Structure, Myth, and Meaning* (Johns Hopkins University Press, 2006)

R.P. Martin, *The Language of Heroes: Speech and Performance in the Iliad* (Cornell University Press, 1989)

M.N. Nagler, *Spontaneity and Tradition: A Study in the Oral Art of Homer* (University of California Press, 1974)

A. Parry (ed.), *The Making of Homeric Verse: The Collected Papers of Milman Parry* (Oxford University Press, 1971)

A. Parry, *The Language of Achilles and Other Papers* (Oxford University Press, 1989)

W.C. Scott, *The Artistry of the Homeric Simile* (Dartmouth College Press, 2009)

Chapter 3. The Hero and Homeric Society

W. Allan and D.L. Cairns, 'Conflict and Community in the *Iliad*', in N. Fisher and H. van Wees (eds), *Competition in the Ancient World* (Classical Press of Wales, 2011) 113-46

D.L. Cairns, *Aidôs: The Psychology and Ethics of Honour and Shame in Ancient Greek Literature* (Oxford University Press, 1993)

M. Clarke, *Flesh and Spirit in the Songs of Homer: A Study of Words and Myths* (Oxford University Press, 1999)

N.R.E. Fisher, *Hybris: A Study in the Values of Honour and Shame in Ancient Greece* (Aris and Phillips, 1992)

D. Hammer, *The Iliad as Politics: The Performance of Political Thought* (University of Oklahoma Press, 2002)

J. Haubold, *Homer's People: Epic Poetry and Social Formation* (Cambridge University Press, 2000)

G. Nagy, *The Best of the Achaeans: Concepts of the Hero in Archaic Greek Poetry*, 2nd edn (Johns Hopkins University Press, 1999)

J. Redfield, *Nature and Culture in the Iliad: The Tragedy of Hector*, 2nd edn (Duke University Press, 1994)

R. Scodel, *Epic Facework: Self-Presentation and Social Interaction in Homer* (Classical Press of Wales, 2008)

S. Scully, *Homer and the Sacred City* (Cornell University Press, 1990)

H. van Wees, *Status Warriors: War, Violence and Society in Homer and History* (J.C. Gieben, 1992)

B. Williams, *Shame and Necessity* (University of California Press, 1993)

Chapter 4. Mortals and Immortals

W. Allan, 'Divine Justice and Cosmic Order in Early Greek Epic', *Journal of Hellenic Studies* 126 (2006) 1-35

W. Burkert, *Greek Religion*, tr. J. Raffan (Blackwell, 1985) 119-25

J. Griffin, *Homer on Life and Death* (Oxford University Press, 1980)

E. Kearns, 'The Gods in the Homeric Epics', in R. Fowler (ed.), *The Cambridge Companion to Homer* (Cambridge University Press, 2004) 59-73

H. Lloyd-Jones, *The Justice of Zeus,* 2nd edn (University of California Press, 1983)

L. Slatkin, *The Power of Thetis: Allusion and Interpretation in the Iliad* (University of California Press, 1992)

M.M. Willcock, 'Some Aspects of the Gods in the *Iliad*', *Bulletin of the Institute of Classical Studies* 17 (1970) 1-10

Chapter 5. War and Family Life

M. Arthur, 'The Divided World of *Iliad* VI', in H.P. Foley (ed.), *Reflections of Women in Antiquity* (Gordon and Breach, 1981) 19-44

M. Clarke, 'Manhood and Heroism', in R. Fowler (ed.), *The Cambridge Companion to Homer* (Cambridge University Press, 2004) 74-90

N. Felson and L. Slatkin, 'Gender and Homeric Epic', in R. Fowler (ed.), *The Cambridge Companion to Homer* (Cambridge University Press, 2004) 91-114

H.P. Foley, 'Women in Ancient Epic', in J.M. Foley (ed.), *A Companion to Ancient Epic* (Blackwell, 2005) 105-18

B. Graziosi and J. Haubold, 'Homeric Masculinity: Ênoreê and Agênoriê', *Journal of Hellenic Studies* 123 (2003) 60-76

W. Schadewaldt, 'Hector and Andromache', in G.M. Wright and P.V. Jones (eds), *Homer: German Scholarship in Translation* (Oxford University Press, 1997) 124-42

H. van Wees, *Greek Warfare: Myths and Realities* (Duckworth, 2004)

Index

—